ILLUSTRATORS 40

THE SOCIETY OF ILLUSTRATORS 40TH
ANNUAL OF AMERICAN ILLUSTRATION

From the exhibition held in the galleries of the
Society of Illustrators Museum of American Illustration
128 East 63rd Street, New York City
February 14-April 18, 1998

Society of Illustrators, Inc.
128 East 63rd Street, New York, NY 10021

ISBN 2-88046-403-X
Library of Congress Catalog Card Number 59-10849

A RotoVision Book
Published and distributed by RotoVision SA
Rue du Bugnon 7
CH-1299 Crans-Pres-Celigny
Switzerland

Tel: +41(22) 776 0511
Fax: +41 (22) 776 0889

RotoVision SA, Sales & Production Office
Sheridan House, 112/116A Western Road
Hove, East Sussex BN3 1DD, UK

Tel. + 44 (0) 1273 72 72 68
Fax + 44 (0) 1273 72 72 69

Cover design by Wendell Minor
Cover painting by Leo & Diane Dillon
Interior design by Bernadette Evangelist

Production and separations in Singapore by ProVision Pte. Ltd.

Tel: +65 334 7720
Fax: +65 334 7721

Photo Credits: Vaughn Andrews by John Johnson, Etienne Delessert by Marcel Imsand, Teresa Fasolino
by Marianne Barcellona, Judy Francis by Harold Hechler, S. Saelig Gallagher by Gene Nocon, Irene Haas
by Anne Saeger, Brad Hamann by Murray Tinkelman, Dean Morrissey by Rebecca A. Brown,
Kadir Nelson (Silver Medal) by Ron Mesaros, Daniel Pelavin by Murray Tinkelman, Jerry Pinkney
by John Lei. Portrait of Anita Kunz by John Collier. Awards Galas photos by George Kanatous.

ILLUSTRATORS 40

THE SOCIETY OF ILLUSTRATORS 40TH

ANNUAL OF AMERICAN ILLUSTRATION

1/40

Published by RotoVision S.A.

THE SOCIETY OF ILLUSTRATORS
40TH ANNUAL EXHIBITION AWARDS GALAS

Editorial & Book, February 13, 1998/Advertising & Institutional, March 20, 1998

John Bergstrom and Joe Sapperson from American Showcase are flanked by Murray Tinkelman, Chairman of the 40th Annual, at left, and Steven Stroud, President of the Society, at right. American Showcase was once again the Exclusive Sponsor of the Annual Exhibition Awards Galas.

Above, a selection of Award Winners who received their medals at each gala. Top, LEFT TO RIGHT: Nancy Leo of Dial Books for Young Readers and Gregory Manchess (Book, Gold); Kadir Nelson (Editorial, Gold) and Andrew Kner of *Scenario* magazine; S. Saelig Gallagher (Editorial, Gold) and Judy Garlan of *The Atlantic Monthly*; Robert Morton of Harry N. Abrams Inc. and Dean Morrissey (Gold, Book). BOTTOM: John Thompson (Book, Gold) and Elizabeth Parisi of Scholastic; Wilson McLean (Gold, Institutional) and Francis Livingston (Silver, Institutional); Grace DeVito (Silver, Advertising), John English (Silver, Institutional), and N. Ascencios (Gold, Institutional); Tom Christopher (Silver, Advertising) and Peter Schaefer, *The New York Times.*

PRESIDENT'S MESSAGE

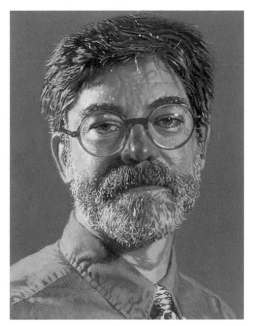

It is the night of February 13, 1998—the gala opening of the 40th Annual Exhibition at the Society's New York headquarters, underwritten by our friends at American Showcase. We are not filled to capacity tonight—we are about two hundred people beyond that—more people than have ever been in the building at one time. The show, as usual, is spectacular. All the current notables of our profession are here—the medal winners, the Hall of Famers. In keeping with our great Call for Entries poster by Leo and Diane Dillon, there is a Jamaican theme—a steel drum plays softly by the gallery bar while waiters serve Caribbean style hors d'oeuvres. Old friendships are renewed. Mutual admirers meet each other. Show Chair Murray T. is there in his traditional black garb and ponytail. He greets only people he knows—everyone. Terry Brown, our

Director, is nervous. He keeps an eye out for the Fire Marshall—a table nearly caught fire earlier in the evening. He ponders how four hundred will fit in our dining room

for the Awards Ceremony. I am to say a few official words of greeting. I am not too nervous—everyone else has done the work. Credit for the success of the evening seems to flow my way, although I had nothing to do with it. The success of the evening came as a result of a dedicated staff, and an enormous group of volunteers, and jurors, headed by the incredibly energetic Murray Tinkelman. Mainly, the success of the show comes from the artists—from the countless hours of work needed to accomplish the art and the dedicated lives that allowed such amazing work to be produced in the first place.

Steven H. Stroud

Steven H. Stroud
President 1997 - 1998

Portrait by John Thompson

CHAIRMAN'S MESSAGE

In 1959, one of the highlights of my year was being asked to be a committee worker on a brand new and rather controversial project being undertaken by the Society of Illustrators. The project, of course, was the premier exhibition of what has become the standard for excellence in our field, the Society of Illustrators Annual of American Illustration.

Time truly does fly, and forty years later serving as Chairman of Illustrators 40 has provided me with a sense of pride and satisfaction that even surpasses that first committee experience.

My Chairman's message is primarily one of thanks—first to Wendell Minor who asked me to serve as his Assistant Chairman for Illustrators 39, which led to my chairmanship of Illustrators 40.

My thanks and admiration to Leo and Diane Dillon, recently elected to the Society of Illustrators Hall of Fame, who

created the wonderful art for the Call for Entries, which was magnificently designed by Wendell Minor.

My thanks and profound respect for the Jury Chairpersons, Joe Ciardiello, Teresa Fasolino, Jerry Pinkney, and Herb Tauss, all

of whom brought a sense of dignity, fairness, and not least of all, collegiality to the judging.

My thanks also to my Assistant Chairman, Vincent DiFate, our most recent Society of Illustrators Past-President, who was my good right hand throughout the proceedings.

Thanks, of course, to the Society's staff headed by Director Terry Brown--they were always there when the going got heavy.

Last and certainly not least, my thanks to Barney Plotkin and his hanging committee, who managed to get all that glorious art on the gallery walls in time for the opening.

Murray Tinkelman

Murray Tinkelman
Chairman, 40th Annual Exhibition

Portrait by John Thompson

ILLUSTRATORS HALL OF FAME

*S*ince 1958, the Society of Illustrators has elected to its Hall of Fame artists recognized for their "distinguished achievement in the art of illustration." The list of previous winners is truly a "Who's Who" of illlustation. Former Presidents of the Society meet annually to elect those who will be so honored.

HALL OF FAME COMMITTEE 1998

Chairman   Murray Tinkelman

Chairman Emeritus   Willis Pyle

Former Presidents   Vincent DiFate

Diane Dillon

Peter Fiore

Charles McVicker

Wendell Minor

Howard Munce

Alvin J. Pimsler

Warren Rogers

Eileen Hedy Schultz

Shannon Stirnweis

David K. Stone

John Witt

HALL OF FAME LAUREATES 1998

Robert M. Cunningham

Frank Frazetta

Boris Artzybasheff*

Kerr Eby*

Edward Penfield*

Martha Sawyers*

HALL OF FAME LAUREATES 1958-1997

1958	Norman Rockwell
1959	Dean Cornwell
1959	Harold Von Schmidt
1960	Fred Cooper
1961	Floyd Davis
1962	Edward Wilson
1963	Walter Biggs
1964	Arthur William Brown
1965	Al Parker
1966	Al Dorne
1967	Robert Fawcett
1968	Peter Helck
1969	Austin Briggs
1970	Rube Goldberg
1971	Stevan Dohanos
1972	Ray Prohaska
1973	Jon Whitcomb
1974	Tom Lovell
1974	Charles Dana Gibson*
1974	N.C. Wyeth*
1975	Bernie Fuchs

1975 Maxfield Parrish*	1983 Noel Sickles*	1992 Joe Bowler
1975 Howard Pyle*	1983 Franklin Booth*	1992 Edwin A. Georgi*
1976 John Falter	1984 Neysa Moran McMein*	1992 Dorothy Hood*
1976 Winslow Homer*	1984 John LaGatta*	1993 Robert McGinnis
1976 Harvey Dunn*	1984 James Williamson*	1993 Thomas Nast*
1977 Robert Peak	1985 Charles Marion Russell*	1993 Coles Phillips*
1977 Wallace Morgan*	1985 Arthur Burdett Frost*	1994 Harry Anderson
1977 J.C. Leyendecker*	1985 Robert Weaver	1994 Elizabeth Shippen Green*
1978 Coby Whitmore	1986 Rockwell Kent*	1994 Ben Shahn*
1978 Norman Price*	1986 Al Hirschfeld	1995 James Avati
1978 Frederic Remington*	1987 Haddon Sundblom*	1995 McClelland Barclay*
1979 Ben Stahl	1987 Maurice Sendak	1995 Joseph Clement Coll*
1979 Edwin Austin Abbey*	1988 René Bouché*	1995 Frank E. Schoonover*
1979 Lorraine Fox*	1988 Pruett Carter*	1996 Herb Tauss
1980 Saul Tepper	1988 Robert T. McCall	1996 Anton Otto Fischer*
1980 Howard Chandler Christy*	1989 Erté	1996 Winsor McCay*
1980 James Montgomery Flagg*	1989 John Held Jr.*	1996 Violet Oakley*
1981 Stan Galli	1989 Arthur Ignatius Keller*	1996 Mead Schaeffer*
1981 Frederic R. Gruger*	1989 Burt Silverman	1997 Leo & Diane Dillon
1981 John Gannam*	1990 Robert Riggs*	1997 Frank McCarthy
1982 John Clymer	1990 Morton Roberts*	1997 Chesley Bonestell*
1982 Henry P. Raleigh*	1991 Donald Teague	1997 Joe DeMers*
1982 Eric (Carl Erickson)*	1991 Jessie Willcox Smith*	1997 Maynard Dixon*
1983 Mark English	1991 William A. Smith*	1997 Harrison Fisher*

Presented posthumously

HALL OF FAME 1998

ROBERT M. CUNNINGHAM (b. 1924)

*I*n a recent *New York Times* review of Robert Cunningham's paintings from the Caribbean, William Zimmer wrote, "... Mr. Cunningham is originally from Kansas, and his native ground has perhaps been an inspiration for the flat, bright planes of color that characterize his work. This insistent abstract component is complemented by a sense of local color, proving that he is on close terms with the place." Zimmer goes on to say that Cunningham shares with Edward Hopper an overwhelming use of light.

For almost forty years Bob Cunningham has made his indelible mark on the field of illustration with his unique sense of abstract composition, color and use of light. He has done so with admirable consistancy for a client list that is the envy of any illustrator: *Sports Illustrated*, DuPont, General Electric, Mobil, Alfa Romeo, AT&T, IBM, American Express, Exxon, American Airlines, ABC, Alcoa, Panasonic, Chevrolet, Mead Paper, Metropolitan Opera, and the U.S. Postal Service. Add to this partial list of clients, Gold and Silver Medals from the Society of Illustrators, as well as the Hamilton King Award in 1983.

One could say that Bob Cunningham has come a long way from Herington, Kansas. The son of a railroad man, Bob was born into a simple life on the heartland prairie. He has two older brothers and a younger sister. His mother died soon after giving birth to his sister in 1929. By the time Bob reached second grade, he had made the decision to become an artist. At age 12, his family moved to Kansas City, Kansas, where Bob graduated from Wyandotte High School in 1942.

He joined the Navy that same year and became an air cadet, finally serving as a radar man in a three-man TBF torpedo bomber. Out of the service in 1945, Bob took advantage of the G.I. Bill and started his studies at the University of Kansas and then went to the Kansas City Art Institute for two years. Bob said recently that had it not been for the G.I. Bill, he may not have had the chance to pursue his artistic dream, proving once again that serendipity plays a pivital role in each of our lives.

In 1949, Bob packed his suitcase and ambition onto a Greyhound bus and headed for New York City. The Art Students League awaited. He was fortunate enough to study under Kuniyoshi, Bosa and Corbino at the League. During this time Bob did plein air painting on the streets of the city.

In 1952, Bob got a job as staff illustrator for a jewelry supply company illustrating various tools used in that industry. His medium was scratchboard, a very exacting medium that bares little resemblence to the Cunningham style that we know today, however, this job served Bob well in that it gave him valuable time and freedom to develop his own sense of personal expression.

Another seminal event in Bob's life occurred at the Art Students League in 1954, while attending a sketchclass. He met Jean Ratley, a talented young fashion illustrator who would become his wife in 1962. Jean has played an important role in Bob's career, offering continued encouragement and an objective voice over these many years.

Bob took a course with Jack Potter at the School of Visual Arts from 1958 to 1959 to which he attributes a change in his perspective on the art of picture making. For the first time Bob felt liberated enough to express himself in a more fluid style.

This set the stage for what Bob calls his big break in illustration: an eight-page portfolio of his work for *Sports Illustrated* assigned by the art director, Richard Gangel. Bob traveled to Canada to record his impressions of a sportsmen's hunt for Canadian geese. The resulting illustrations were a great success. His second big break was a dream assignment for any illustrator: create art for an Aqueduct horse racing poster. Bob had total freedom to do whatever he wanted, as long as he didn't show the horses from behind. The final poster won a Gold Medal at the Society's annual exhibition.

These initial "breaks" for Bob have become our good fortune. We have been witness to his exceptional contributions to the field of illustration for four decades. Bob's genius has been his ability to be himself: the man from the plains of Kansas who creates deceptively simple pictures that delight the eye. His pictures are timeless, and therefore will stand the test of time. Bob's honesty and humbleness are refreshing in these over-promoted and over-hyped times. Maybe it's because Bob has the soul of a fine artist who knows where he is going, and is always willing to learn and challenge his beliefs. Whatever the reason, Bob Cunningham has made the world of illustration a better place, and we are all the better for it.

Wendell Minor
Past President, Society of
Illustrators, 1989-91
Hall of Fame Committee

Red Fin Fish, an illustration for Art Director Harvey Grut of *Sports Illustrated* for a piece about fishing in Argentina. Mohawk Graphics Collection.

HALL OF FAME 1998

FRANK FRAZETTA (b.1924)

*T*he work of Frank Frazetta is as atypical as his approach to it. Unlike most artists, Frazetta prefers to work in a vacuum, free of influences and unencumbered by reality. He creates a new world with each painting and doesn't want facts (what's so) to interfere with fiction (what isn't so). That way his magical brush can bridge the span between two diametrically opposed perceptions.

With only his imagination as reference, Frazetta paints with such persuasive accuracy that the viewer often accepts one of his landscapes as if it were the camera's vision. And it is executed with such craft that none can doubt the artist had painted that vista on-the-spot, regardless of its inter-planetary location.

How he reached the level of excellence and acceptance that made him the dominant artist of his genre is a question that addresses Frazetta's natural drawing ability and not his formal art education, since he had none of the latter as an adult. Brooklyn born and raised, as a youth Frazetta displayed an astonishing talent for drawing. Between the ages of eight and twelve, he attended private painting lessons from a local artist. That proved to be the only training he experienced. All that followed can be accurately labeled "self-taught."

His early years as a cartoonist proved invaluable to the development of his phenomenal visual imagination. At age sixteen his animated comics caught the attention of the Walt Disney Studios, but Frazetta never considered leaving the neighborhood baseball diamonds where his exploits were also catching the attention of professional scouts. At nineteen, Frazetta was named Most Valuable Player of the Parade Grounds League, a highly regarded minor league. He burned up the league with a .487 batting average.

Despite baseball sharing equal pas-

sion, it was his art that Frazetta knew would be his life's work. It was more a rational decision than an emotional one. Factoring in equal success as a professional at the top of each of the respective fields, he'd obviously enjoy more longevity as an artist while still having fun as an athlete. His legions of fans and followers still applaud his decision.

As he became more involved in the representational comic form, Frazetta realized that his extraordinary drawing skill alone wasn't enough to satisfy his need as a storyteller. Exaggerated action, dramatic lighting, dynamic composition, and an imaginative and highly personal color sense all played a part in depicting the quintessential moment of a larger-than-life scene that became his illustration hallmark.

Frazetta's career exploded when at long last the perfect subject matter was given to the perfect artist to depict it. Starting with new editions of Edgar Rice Burrough's Tarzan adventures, Ace Publishers were ecstatic with the success of their series brandishing Frazetta covers. Lancer Books enjoyed similar success with their own Conan the Barbarian series.

The Society of Illustrators gave Frank Frazetta an Award of Excellence in their 15th Annual Exhibition of American Illustration.

To Frazetta, the blank canvas is not a proving ground for his remarkable ability as much as it is an undiscovered planet to explore—a place to discover what imagery it has to offer. When not bridled with an actual subject to depict, as a book cover, for example, he will begin a new work "somewhere in the middle" of an action, mood, or composition, either referring to a quick thumbnail sketch representing his first pass at storytelling, or by letting his imagination guide the path of his light pencil work or direct thinned oil line. As in all his art, Frazetta maintains no set work procedure, relying on mood, music, or whim to determine that day's approach. From these minute beginnings evolve works that appear to have been labored over for many months, despite the fact that most were completed overnight, others within two or three days.

Materials have always been held with minimal consideration by the artist. Many of his bristle and sable brushes date before the oldest of his four children was born, still serviceable by Frazetta's standards, despite the wear. More amazing is the watercolor set used to execute all of his early work in that medium. Also still in use today, Frazetta is concerned that nothing currently available in stores "match the vibrancy of that Mickey Mouse 12-color set" he has cherished all these years

Obviously, the art of Frank Frazetta has little to do with methods and techniques and all to do with natural talent. The ability to transform the unbelievable and abstract into imagery both believable and accessible can't be taught. Only imitated. And, as usual in the case of those often imitated, never equaled.

Nick Meglin

The Death Dealer, oil, 1973, collection of the artist.

HALL OF FAME 1998

BORIS ARTZYBASHEFF (1899-1965)

"*G*et out of Russia, don't sponge on my reputation, and change your name." These were words of advice offered by M.P. Artsybasev, a well known and respected Russian author, to his son Boris shortly before the first world war. Born in 1899, in Kharkov, Ukraine, the younger Artzybasheff did not leave Russia until 1919 after the Russian Revolution. After a long and often harrowing journey the young artist finally settled in New York City where he embarked on his career. His earliest employment was as an engraver designing labels for beer and medicine bottles, but Artzybasheff began doing free-lance work and soon established a reputation for creative design. Some of his early commissions included newspaper illustrations, stage designs for the Ziegfeld Theater and Michael Fokine's Russian Ballet, and a mural for a 57th Street speakeasy.

Eventually Artzybasheff turned his attention to illustrating books for publishers in New York and Paris. In 1927 his book designs won him the first of many prestigious awards including best illustrated book from both the American Library Association (the John Newberry Award) and the American Institute of Graphic Arts. Throughout his career Artzybasheff was commissioned to design more than thirty books and illustrate another twenty, including several children's books. Scratchboard, woodcut and wood engraving were popular media used by illustrators for book reproductions but presented challenges to both the artist and the publisher when color was desired. Artzybasheff adopted a technique that incorporated the use of transparent pyroxylin plastic as his matrix because it allowed sharp, precise line quality and easy registration of multi-

ple blocks or colors. This process was used for several award-winning designs by Artzybasheff during the late 1920s and the 1930s.

In 1940 the editors of *Fortune* commissioned Artzybasheff to design a cover for the magazine. The artist had already created several colorful graphs and charts to illustrate articles in the magazine when he submitted a painting of a Japanese soldier standing before a large sculpted head of the Buddha. This cover art attracted the attention of *Time* magazine editors who were assembling a staff of illustrators to create their cover designs. Before his death in 1965 Artzybasheff created more than 200 covers for *Time* including portraits of Stalin, Hitler, Truman, Mao Tse Tung, and Ho Chi Minh.

Other compelling forms of Artzybasheff's published art were his paintings and drawings of humanized machines and mechanized humans. These pictures, which often border on the surreal, display a keen sense of how the machine works or what human task the machine was meant to

replace. The images of animated weapons of war and tyranny that were created for *Life* magazine demonstrate how men can create monsters that are real and deadly. When asked about his thoughts on war and weaponry, Artzybasheff replied, *"I try to shake this thought off: It may be that a healthy planet should have no more life upon it than a well-kept dog has fleas; but what possesses the flea to concoct its own flea powder?"* According to the editors of *Life*, Artzybasheff war machines "take a sardonic delight in their own powers of destruction." Many of his anthropomorphic designs, along with numerous other illustrations, were published in his 1954 book, *As I See*.

Artzybasheff approached the creation of his paintings with an attention to detail and process that was similar to an engineer's approach to designing a machined component. The precision of the planned design and his control over the methods and materials were extremely important to Artzybasheff. He kept extensive notes on his ideas, technique, and formulae for mixing gouache paints, and even notated his preparatory sketches, constantly making revisions and adaptations. Often, Artzybasheff would "build" his paintings, starting with detailed drawings (he called them "skeletons") that were layered with "skins" of color to develop the final design of the painting. Components or features were frequently designed separately and then brought to the composition in their final form. The final result was a picture that displayed the unique and imaginative vision of an artist who was justifiably labeled the "Master of the Machine Age."

Domenic J. Iacono
Associate Director
Syracuse University
Art Collection

Foreign Correspondent, 1964, gouache on board, 19 3/4 x 15 3/4 inches. Courtesy of the Syracuse University Art Collection.

HALL OF FAME 1998

KERR EBY (1889-1946)

Kerr Eby would probably consider it a compliment to be cited as being different from most commercial illustrators of his time. One aspect of his career which set him apart from others was his ability to, as Dorothy Noyes Arms writes in *American Etchers* vol. viii, "[see] straight into the heart of the subject." Generally, this type of vision is not associated with commercial success for mainstream illustrators. Yet limited commercial success didn't hamper Eby's enthusiastic passion for his work—Arms goes on to call his work "essentially individualistic" with every etching plate "express[ing] his forceful personality and complete sincerity.

Over the course of his career, Eby's work transformed from direct, on-the-spot depictions of events to capturing the essence of the subject, thus making it more universally applicable. As Arms wrote in 1929: "One feels the soul which inhabits the inanimate as well as the animate object." Evolving from direct interpretation to the jelling of observation over time took a period of years. Writing of the subjects produced during Eby's involvement in World War I, Arms goes on to say:"They were etched when the horror and nobleness, ruin and tragic beauty of it all were fresh and vivid things in Mr. Eby's memory. Then came the reaction against all reminders of those days, and peaceful scenes and tranquil subjects held sway, until now, in 1929, there appears a new war plate....It is war itself, seen through the eyes of an artist, and reproduced for all time by his most skilful hand."

Eby's work cannot be sufficiently appreciated without some background on his experiences in the two world wars. Before the United States' entry into the First World War, Eby volunteered for the Ambulance Corps, sketching scenes of the front during breaks in the action. Over the course of his duties most sketches were lost, "but," according to Eby's profile in *A Community of Artists, Westport—Weston 1900-1985* by Dorothy and John Tarrant, "the

scenes were stored in his memory." George Wright, a close friend during later years wrote: "Other artists did good work. None of them had the feeling of the pains, agonies and dirt of war as he sensed them." Eby distilled his impressions of World War I into his landmark book *War*, published in 1936. Its publication was arguably the pinnacle of Eby's career.

Kerr Eby was born in 1889 in Japan, the son of Canadian Methodist missionaries. The family returned to Canada in about 1891, moving to New York City in 1907. The young Eby attended Pratt Institute and the Art Students League before joining the American Lithography Company.

When America entered World War I Eby, already overseas with the Ambulance Corps, was assigned to camouflage detail. There he met Robert Lawson, later his Connecticut neighbor. Eby moved to Westport in the late 1910s and his non-war work quickly fell under the influence of Connecticut scenery. Despite a comfortable life in his pre-Revolutionary War house "Driftway," much of Eby's work still focussed on war subjects. As time went on he vocally opposed the United States' contemplated entrance into World War II, writing in *War*: "I am a very profane man. I am not being profane when I say `For Christ's sake, say or do what you can! [to

stop the war]."'

Of course, the strength of Eby's convictions aside, the United States entered the war. In 1943, Eby shipped off to the Pacific theatre as an artist-correspondent for Abbott Laboratories. Again, he lived at the front, recording in human terms the battles of Tarawa and New Britain among others. Upon his return in March 1944 he continued his work for Abbott, culminating in *Marines in Action*.

Eby was praised by the Marines, despite his longstanding anti-war sentiments. As Major General Julian Smith wrote of Eby's work in *Marines in Action*: "They have caught the dramatic intensity and the spirit of men at war, the very feeling of the man in battle, the sludging through the jungle and the terrible murky heat, the charge on the pillbox, the savagery, the terror, the exhaustion of battle. Kerr Eby has made a great contribution to the war. The Marines, and I believe, no less the public, are in his debt. If he had somewhere expressed a high opinion of the Marines, let us for our part make public declaration that it is mutual, both for the life he lived among us and for the work here represented." This is strong praise, particularity aimed, as it was, at someone who wrote and published the statement: "I am certainly a pacifist if being one is to believe that lawful, not to say sanctified, wholesale murder is simply slobbering imbecility." Whatever the subject, whatever the medium, Eby expressed himself clearly and succinctly.

Though Eby's talents are often under-appreciated today, there are many opportunities to see why he belongs in the Society's Hall of Fame, in addition to modest holdings in its Permanent Collection. His work is represented in depth in the Navy Combat Art Collection, the Marine Corps Museum, and the Prints Collection of the New York Public Library.

Frederic B. Taraba

Refueling in Burma, WWII, charcoal, Permanent Collection of the Society of Illustrators Museum of American Illustration.

HALL OF FAME 1998

EDWARD PENFIELD (1866-1925)

America has produced many excellent poster artists, but Edward Penfield must surely be placed at the top of the list. A precocious talent, he was still a student at the Art Students League under the tutelage of George deForest Brush when his work in a school exhibition was seen by the art editor of *Harper's* magazine. Penfield was offered a staff job in the art department and thrived on the on-the-job training. When a poster deadline came due, Penfield volunteered to fill the breach and overnight produced the first of a long series of distinctive posters that made Penfield's reputation as the father of the American Poster Movement.

Many sources can be seen in his work, certainly that of Lautrec and Steinlen in Paris, The Beggarstaff Brothers (James Pryde and William Nicholson) of England, and the Japanese Ukiyo-E woodblock prints. Penfield also acknowledged the influence of the early Egyptian sarcophagi paintings. After becoming the art editor, Penfield was also a strong supporter of other artists' work. For instance, he invited William Nicholson from England and even provided him with space to work in his *Harper's* office.

However, his poster style was his own, characterized by strong shapes simplified to the barest essentials and with elements selected that were of impeccable taste and draftsmanship. The simplification of detail was essential to the success

of a poster which had to be immediately apprehended by a casual passerby. This same requirement applied to magazine covers as they were displayed in competition with other publications. Penfield's cover designs were, therefore, conceived as miniposters that more than held their own on the newsstands.

After his stint with *Harper's*—during which he served as art editor for *Harper's Weekly* and *Monthly*, as well as *Harper's Bazar* (1891-1901), he struck out on his own. His first free-lance assignment took him to Holland, leading to a series of articles on Dutch life, which he both wrote and illustrated. Later combined into a book, *Holland Sketches*, in 1907; they were a great success. This was followed in 1911 by a similar project during which he traveled throughout Spain and his Spanish Sketches were

equally successful.

Upon his return to the United States, he became a regular contributor of covers to *The Saturday Evening Post*, *Collier's*, the old *Life* magazine, *Harper's Weekly*, *Literary Digest*, *The Country Gentleman*, and *Metropolitan Magazine*. He was also an effective designer of calendars. His annual designs for the Beck Engraving Company were prized by other artists and saved long after the calendar years had expired.

Penfield was particularly interested in early coaches and other horse-drawn vehicles and often used them as picture themes. He could draw upon his own collection of stage coaches—a one-horse shay and other vehicles, along with saddles and harness which occupied his "museum" on the ground floor under his studio.

Penfield contributed his work to further the American cause during World War I, creating many effective posters. He was also active in other public service roles through his membership in the Society of Illustrators, where he served as president; The Art Center; The Guild of Free Lance Artists; and the American Watercolor Society. He also taught at the Art Students League.

As we review Penfield's work from the perspective of three-quarters of a century, it has a timeless quality that could be published as well today and should only look better in the future.

Walt Reed
Illustration House

Poster Calendar 1897, published by R.H. Russell & Son, New York. Courtesy of Ilustration House.

HALL OF FAME 1998
MARTHA SAWYERS (1902-1986)

Standing a scant five feet, Martha Sawyers' small frame belied a spirit as boundless as the Texas plains where she spent her childhood. Born in Corsicana in 1902, her expansive home state could not contain her ambitions. As a child she dreamed, drew, and read. Though her favorite volume, *Religions of the Far East*, must have seemed an unlikely choice for a child, the book sparked a life-long interest in Asian culture and fed her wanderlust. By the age of seventeen she was ready to leave home.

In 1919 Sawyers headed east to New York City. She supported herself by working at the stained glass studio of J&R Lamb while she studied at the Art Students League. There she met her future husband William Reusswig—a student of promising ability with a spirit of adventure that matched her own. She was fortunate in her teachers. George Luks taught her to paint with sensitivity, and George Bridgman emphasized the fluent drawing style that was to become her hallmark. Sixty-five years later, when asked about her education, she remembered, "I studied with the best teachers until they kicked me out and said I had to do something with what I knew."

Martha Sawyers followed their advice and left school. Although she maintained her position at J&R Lamb, her interest in seeking out unusual subjects for portraiture led her to the haunts of the actors and musicians who flocked to New York in the heady twenties. Her work attracted favorable attention, and she secured a job drawing portraits for the Theater Section of the *New York Herald Tribune*. Other commissions followed. By 1928, she and William Reusswig were both successful illustrators. They married but didn't settle down. Both longed to see the world, "to see beyond the bend in the river."

In the mid-thirties the pair embarked

on a world tour that included travel in Europe, China, Japan, and Bali. During their wanderings Sawyers rekindled her childhood fascination with the Far East and was captivated by the people she met in Asia. Compassionate and vivacious, she rarely had any problem finding models. The couple assimilated easily into the indigenous culture and adopted the habit of donning local clothing as soon as they arrived in a new area. As William Reusswig wrote years later, "Buying native clothing and wearing it on the spot isn't such a bad idea. Maybe people are laughing at you, but *they're laughing*."

When she returned to New York in 1937, Martha Sawyers was carrying a large portfolio of expressive portraits. She exhibited the work at the Marie Sterner Gallery, where it met with both critical and popular success. William Chessman, art editor of *Collier's*, was impressed and began to send Sawyers assignments. Notable among her commissions were paintings for three serialized novels by Pearl Buck. Although her output for *Collier's* was prodigious, that publication was not her only client. Sawyers' illustrations also appeared in *Liberty*, *American*, and *Life* and on two posters in support of China Relief.

During the war years, Sawyers and Reusswig both accepted assignments as artist correspondents. Reusswig went to Europe, and Sawyers was the only artist *Collier's* sent to Asia. From Burma, India, and China she sent back stories and drawings. Her favorite subjects were common people elevated to heroism by events beyond their control. There was a haunting portrait of fourteen-year-old La Waang Gam, a Burmese sharpshooter who defended his country with honor although his short arms prevented him from ever reaching the forward grip of his gun. There was a portrait of Anna Chow, a Chinese doctor with a spirit that matched Sawyers' own. Chow tended the sick and wounded during the worst of the Japanese bombing. Anna's next challenge, Sawyers wrote, "is to make one parachute jump. No one seems to know why."

The end of the war did not mark the end of Sawyers' travels. In 1956 the couple made a final trip to Asia, returning home with enough material for two books; *India and South East Asia* was published in 1961, followed by *The Illustrated Book About the Far East* in 1964. Reusswig's declining health precipitated the couple's final journey—from their home in New Milford, Connecticut, to retirement in San Antonio, Texas. Reusswig died in 1978 and Sawyers in 1986.

Throughout her remarkable career, Sawyers lived a life of freedom and adventure that few women had the fortitude or the opportunity to emulate. Two years before her death, on the occasion of a retrospective show of her work, a reporter asked Martha Sawyers about her nomadic life. "Did I enjoy it?" Sawyers replied. "Oh, I had a hell of a good time."

Alice "Bunny" Carter
College of Humanities
and the Arts
San Jose State University

China Sky, oil on canvas, illustration from "China Sky" by Pearl S. Buck, *Collier's*, March 1, 1941. Permanent Collection of the Society of Illustrators Museum of American Illustration.

THE HAMILTON KING AWARD

The Hamilton King Award, created by Mrs. Hamilton King in memory of her husband through a bequest, is presented annually for the best illustration of the year by a member of the Society. The selection is made by former recipients of this award and may be won only once.

Also, the Society of Illustrators presents Special Awards each year for substantial contributions to the profession. The Dean Cornwell Recognition Award honors someone for past service which has proven to have been an important contribution to the Society. The Arthur William Brown Achievement Award honors someone who has made a substantial contribution to the Society over a period of time.

HAMILTON KING AWARD 1965-1998

1965	Paul Calle
1966	Bernie Fuchs
1967	Mark English
1968	Robert Peak
1969	Alan E. Cober
1970	Ray Ameijide
1971	Miriam Schottland
1972	Charles Santore
1973	Dave Blossom
1974	Fred Otnes
1975	Carol Anthony
1976	Judith Jampel
1977	Leo & Diane Dillon
1978	Daniel Schwartz
1979	William Teason
1980	Wilson McLean
1981	Gerald McConnell
1982	Robert Heindel
1983	Robert M. Cunningham
1984	Braldt Bralds
1985	Attila Hejja
1986	Doug Johnson
1987	Kinuko Y. Craft
1988	James McMullan
1989	Guy Billout
1990	Edward Sorel
1991	Brad Holland
1992	Gary Kelley
1993	Jerry Pinkney
1994	John Collier
1995	C.F. Payne
1996	Etienne Delessert
1997	Marshall Arisman
1998	Jack Unruh

SPECIAL AWARDS 1998

1998 ARTHUR WILLIAM BROWN ACHIEVEMENT AWARD

Dilys Evans

*T*he idea for a show of the fine art of children's books was born while Dilys Evans was working at *Cricket Magazine* as assistant art director. Seeing the original art, in contrast to the printed piece, she felt the originals should be seen by more people. At that time, in the early 1970s, children's book illustration was not fully appreciated. With art director Trina Schart Hyman, Dilys established a traveling exhibition of art created for the magazines.

In 1977 Dilys moved to New York and established Dilys Evans Fine Illustration representing illustrators. Her background as an art director and as an artist (she apprenticed with Nell Blaine, studied at the Art Students League, The New School, and exhibited at the Green Mountain Gallery for four years) gave her the unique understanding of the creative process and the practical matters of business. Artists she has represented speak highly of her compassion and concern for the direction in which they wish their careers to go—even if it means turning away work.

Dilys was determined to find a site to host an exhibit of children's book art along with the printed books. In 1978 she met Clarence Bayliss, Director of public relations for the Master Eagle Printing Group. Thus began the annual exhibition which was held at the Master Eagle Gallery. It was at that time we got to know Dilys and exhibited our work at the gallery each year.

When the Master Eagle Gallery closed, Dilys searched for a permanent home for the exhibit and found it at the Society of Illustrators. Since 1989, the show has continued to grow both in entries and prestige and is one of the Society's most successful shows. In addition to wall-to-wall attendance at the openings, there is a panel on some aspect of children's book publishing during the exhibit.

Dilys remains active in supporting illustration. She is guest speaker and panelist at colleges around the country, reviews portfolios, has curated exhibits at The Muscarelle Museum in Virginia, The Memorial Art Gallery in New York, The New Britain Museum of American Art, has written numerous articles and two children's books.

This award is most deserved for Dilys's dedication to the art of children's books and to the illustrators. We congratulate her.

Leo & Diane Dillon

1998 DEAN CORNWELL RECOGNITION AWARD

Bradbury Thompson

*T*he letters **SI** appear at first to be the phonetic spelling of the word sigh. Not so. They're the characters of the Society's logo. However, it is with a sigh to remember that its creator is no longer with us.

Bradbury Thompson's bringing together of these two graphically opposite letter forms is as fresh today as it was when it was conceived 35 years ago. The letters work in black and white. They dazzle in red and black!

Brad was one of the most important designers of the 20th century. That's no puffed-up encomium; here's a partial unpadded list of some of his accomplishments...art director, *Mademoiselle*...design director of *Art News* and *Annual*...redesign of three dozen formats for other magazines including *Smithsonian*...several limited edition books...120 United States Postage stamps...many corporate identity programs and logos...19 years working with the Citizens' Stamp Advisory Committee...design of the superlative Washburn College Bible (you won't find many other Society members with biblical credits on their resumes).

One of Brad's greatest achievements was his design of over 60 issues of *Westvaco Inspirations*, a remarkable accomplishment of graphic invention, wit, color, and press excellence. It was distributed to thousands of printers, designers, and teachers to show the range and versatility of printing papers.

Nobody ever discarded a copy. Even mothers who unknowingly chucked out their sons' baseball cards and collections of *Mad* magazine and Superman comics to neaten up the attic kept hands off.

Brad lived to be 84 and in those years he received just about every design honor extant; and during 30 of those years he taught at the Yale School of Art. His students were worshippers.

He was a handsome, soft-spoken man when he chose to speak...mostly he was a courteous listener. As anyone who ever put their stamp designs before him for evaluation can attest, he would silently appraise them while you stood there and grew roots to the floor awaiting his considered decision.

But you knew that there was no ego involved, just cool calculation. This was a man who knew his A B C's. He was one of the best friends our alphabet ever had.

Besides, he was an elegant gent.

Howard Munce
Honorary President

HAMILTON KING AWARD 1998

JACK UNRUH (b.1935)

When I was asked by the editor if I would write this piece, I began to reflect on a person whom I have known for many years. I realized that I have been the benefactor of a long-standing friendship with a man whose work I admire more than I am able to put into a few words on this page.

I first met Jack Unruh in 1965, when he reviewed my school portfolio in his studio in Dallas. I was impressed and surprised to find that he worked in a tie, button-down shirt, and wing-tipped shoes. Clean shaven with a crew cut, Jack was very much the executive-looking artist. Most of you know that he long ago traded in the wing tips for sneakers and has grown a beard, but his appearance is incidental to the one thing that impressed me most about Jack back then and still does today. I was amazed at his incredible drawing ability, which has been the foundation for not only one, but two very successful illustration styles that he has perfected over the years. Jack is the only artist I know who excels in both a realistic pen-and-ink approach as well as his whimsical, off-the-wall style, using the same tools for each.

Jack frequently will work on projects in both styles simultaneously, doing finished art on an outdoor piece for *National Geographic*, while developing ideas for another client that might feature his funny little "jesters" in some obscene configuration, all beautifully designed and well thought out. When I asked him to talk about the two styles, he said that "one is reflecting upon an image and developing it," while the other "is something you find within your imagination and draw it out." Maybe that part goes back to the time when, as a boy growing up in Pretty Prairie, Kansas, Jack remembers listening to the radio and drawing the images that would come into his mind. In any case, his remarkable draftsmanship is at the center

of both approaches and has given Jack a flexibility that most illustrators only dream about.

The Hamilton King Award is certainly a career honor for any and all who have received it. Jack's reaction to winning it: "I was a tad bit surprised," is typical of the modest way he looks at his work. Jack refers to the piece as "one of those jobs with hardly any money but complete freedom to do whatever you want." Part of a promotional booklet for a printer, Baker Press, the assignment called for illustrating the concept of "one-half." The bearded magician and his female assistant are typical characters from Jack's whimsical bag of tricks. Also characteristic are the small details that lend so much to his work...the hundreds of pen strokes that make up the grain in the floorboards, the fabrics, the curtain detailing, the girl's teeth, the costumes, the pigeon taking a bow...all in a beautifully designed composition that looks like it might have taken a month to produce. Far from it—Jack rarely takes more than three or four days for such a piece.

Jack is also one of the most prolific illustrators I have ever known...no, he IS the most prolific. About ten years ago, he

and I came up with the idea of creating a "garage sale" or "yard sale" with artwork that had been accumulating in our closets...not good enough to frame or exhibit, but too good to throw away. With something affordable to anyone, it was a big success. So we try to have one every two or three years. While it takes that long for me to accumulate enough drawings, sketches, comps, and paintings to cover a couple of tables, Jack will have many boxes stuffed full of his artwork that easily fills several tables in the area behind his studio that we use for the sale. I'm always in awe of the amount of artwork he produces while managing to take time for frequent fishing and hunting trips along the way.

Jack received his BFA in illustration from Washington University in St. Louis and began his career in a studio in Dallas, where he and his wife, Judy, still live. He has been well represented in every Society of Illustrators Annual Exhibition since 1967, having won both Gold and Silver Medals. As one would expect, his client list is impressive and lengthy, including all of the major magazines and hundreds of major American and foreign corporations. Jack taught illustration at East Texas State University for many years and conducts workshops in the summer at the Illustration Academy in Kansas.

I know that my own work has often benefited from his suggestions and from just being around someone as enthusiastic about his work as Jack is. He has been my model for a good many illustrations (especially when I need a fisherman), and the one person who is always willing to share a beer and compare notes about our sometimes frustrating business. As I said when I began this writing, the words here could never adequately express my real admiration and respect for the work of this truly one-of-a-kind artist and friend.

Bart Forbes

1/2 Off Theme, for Baker Press, ink and watercolor on illustration board.

SOCIETY OF ILLUSTRATORS

ILLUSTRATORS 40

THE SOCIETY OF ILLUSTRATORS 40TH
ANNUAL OF AMERICAN ILLUSTRATION

EDITORIAL JURY

Herb Tauss
Chairman, Illustrator

Bob Dacey
Illustrator

Alice Degenhardt
Design Director, PW Communications Group

Leo Dillon
Illustrator

Barbara Fitzsimmons
William Morrow Co.

Donato Giancola
Illustrator

Michell Hooks
Illustrator

Carol Porter-Esmailpour
Art Director, The Washington Post

Bill Sienkiewicz
Illustrator

EDITORIAL

AWARD
WINNERS

S. SAELIG GALLAGHER
Gold Medal

TONY LANE
Gold Medal

KADIR NELSON
Gold Medal

N. ASCENCIOS
Silver Medal

GREG SPALENKA
Silver Medal

KENT WILLIAMS
Silver Medal

I

Artist: **S. Saelig Gallagher**

Art Director: Judy Garlan

Client: The Atlantic Monthly

Medium: Mixed on ragboard

Size: 11" x 20"

"A rope tied from porch post to barn door was the only means of finding one's way through the blinding storm described in 'Horse Heaven Hills.' When Art Director Judy Garland and I discussed the manuscript, our descent into the folds of the story led to an inevitable sympathy for the intense isolation and struggle of this scene. I was struck by the simplicity and poetic potential of a figure wrapped in wind. Visually I wanted to articulate the figure's distress, her precarious and thwarted movement, the mass of her form weighing heavily against the atmospheric structure of the composition."

2

Artist: **Tony Lane**

Art Director: Tony Lane

Client: Forbes ASAP

Medium: Acrylic on canvas

Tony Lane is an eclectic, semi-dyslexic Jewish, Christian, Buddhist monk living as a part-time hermit in the foothills of Oakland, California. His painting was included in the Forbes ASAP because the writer, George Gilder, needed an elephant and Tony just happened to have one rolled up in his closet. He has run numerous art departments, including those of Rolling Stone, Elektra/Asylum Records, and Sony Music/CBS Records. He is Forbes ASAP's art director.

3

Artist: **Kadir Nelson**

Art Director: Andrew Kner

Client: Scenario Magazine

Medium: Oil on canvas

Size:: 14" x 23"

"Andy Kner and I both agreed that I shouldn't see the film before I started painting. He thought it better that I create my own vision for the story. I think any artist can appreciate that. In this piece I wanted to capture the heat of the anger of the approaching mob. It is also an homage to N.C. Wyeth."

4

Artist: **N. Ascencios**

Art Director: Katie Craig

Client: The American Benefactor/Impres, Inc.

Medium: Oil on canvas

Size: 20" x 15"

"She plays with Form."

5

Artist: **Greg Spalenka**

Art Directors: Jay Colton, Marti Golon

Client: Time Digital

Medium: Digital

Size: 10" x 20"

"For the past sixteen years I have asked myself, 'Can Illustration sustain me?' Every year has been a lesson in the blessings and curses of freelance. Freedom and uncertainty. Fortunately the freedom has far outweighed the uncertainty, becoming a catalyst to create new opportunities, especially during lean times. These opportunities have expanded my personal vision as an artist, and continue to sustain me in my creative livelihood."

6

Artist: **Kent Williams**

Art Director: Tom Staebler

Client: Playboy

Medium: Mixed

Size: 18" x 27"

"Author: Mickey Spillane. Title: Black Alley...this was a great opportunity to do illustration as straight-up illustration. No threats of higher concepts here. Just straightforward picture making—guns ablazing!"

7

Artist: **Herb Tauss**
Medium: Oil on canvas
Size: 31" x 23"

8

Artist: **Bill James**
Medium: Pastels on watercolor board

9

Artist: **Susan Leopold**
Art Director: Marci Schultz
Client: Discipleship Journal
Medium: Mixed, collage
Size: 14" x 16"

10

Artist: **Michael Whelan**
Medium: Acrylic on board

11

Artist: **Brad Holland**
Art Directors: Frank DeVino, Nick Torell
Client: Penthouse
Medium: Acrylic on masonite
Size: 11" x 17"

7

8

9

10

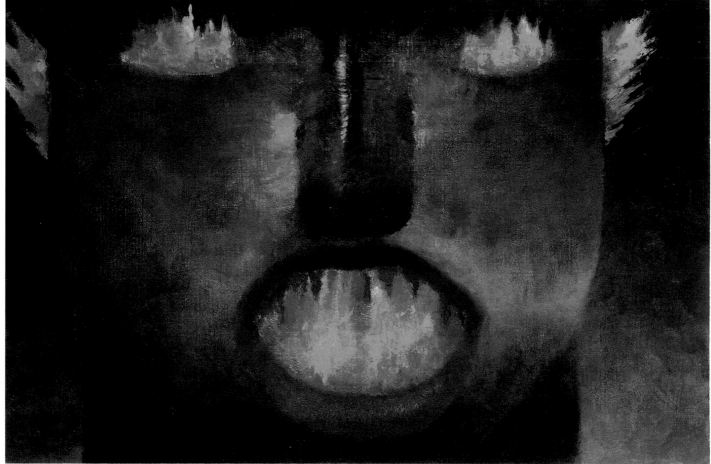

11

12

Artist: **Greg Spalenka**

Art Priscilla Henderer

Client: Rutka Weadock

Medium: Mixed

Size: 12" x 7"

13

Artist: **Greg Spalenka**

Art Directors: Jay Colton, Marti Golon

Client: Public Time Digital

Medium: Digital

Size : 11" x 12"

14

Artist: **Marshall Arisman**

Art Director: Steve Heller

Client: The New York Times Book Review

Medium: Oil on ragboard

Size: 16" x 13"

15

Artist: **Tim O'Brien**

Art Director: Arthur Hochstein, Kenneth Smith

Client: Time

Medium: Oil on board

Size: 9" x 8"

16

Artist: **Richard Schlecht**

Art Director: Chris Sloan

Client: National Geographic

Medium: Watercolor, ink on paper

Size:: 17" x 13"

12

13

14

15

16

17

Artist: **Theo Rudnak**

Art Director: Judy Garlan

Client: The Atlantic Monthly

Medium: Gouache on Strathmore ragboard

Size: 13" x 10"

18

Artist: **Anita Kunz**

Art Director: Samantha Hand

Client: Wake Forest

Medium: Mixed on board

Size: 10" x 7"

19

Artist: **Brad Holland**

Art Director: Rockwell Harwood

Client: Esquire

Medium: Acrylic on masonite

Size: 11" x 10"

20

Artist: **Joseph Daniel Fiedler**

Art Director: Ken McFarlin

Client: The New York Times Magazine/
The Sophisticated Traveler

Medium: Alkyd on paper

Size: 8" x 11"

17

18

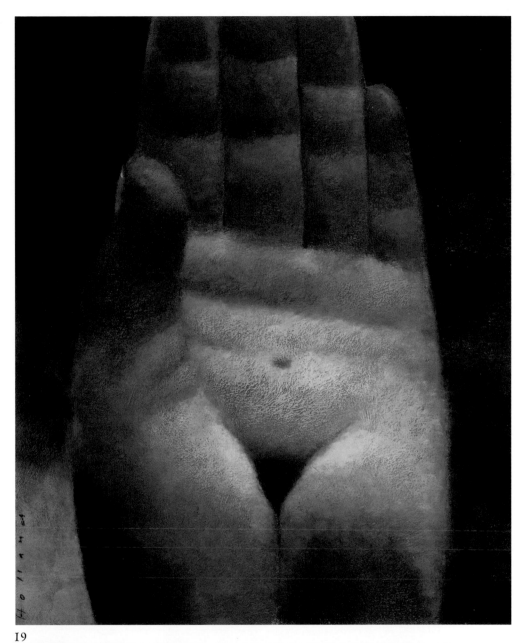

19

20

21

Artist: **Bill Koeb**

Art Director: Scott Clum

Client: Ray-Gun Publishing

Medium: Mixed, digital

Size: 9" x 9"

22

Artist: **Greg Spalenka**

Art Director: Elaine Bradley

Client: Harvard Magazine

Medium: Mixed, digital

23

Artist: **N. Ascencios**

Art Director: Andrea Dunham

Client: New York

Medium: Oil on canvas

Size: 11" x 11"

24

Artist: **N. Ascencios**

Art Directors: Florian Bachleda,
              Andrea Dunham

Client: New York

Medium: Oil on canvas

Size 13" x 10"

25

Artist: **N. Ascencios**

Art Directors: Florian Bachleda,
              Andrea Dunham

Client: New York

Medium: Oil on canvas

Size: 13" x 10"

21

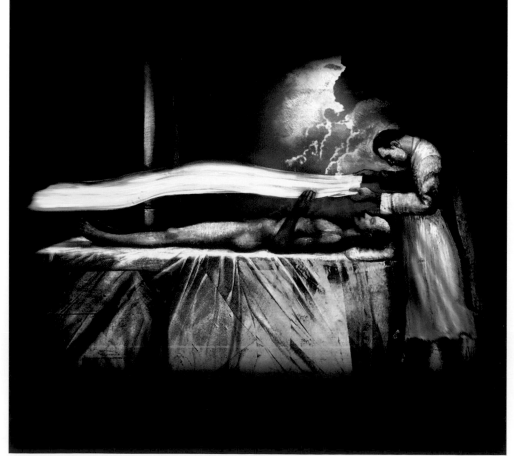

22

23

24

25

26

Artist: **Julie Delton**

Art Director: Ellen Winkler

Client: The Chronicle of Higher Education

Medium: Watercolor, inks, collage on paper

Size: 2" x 9"

27

Artist: **Phil Boatwright**

Art Director: Greg Breeding

Client: Worldwide Challenge Magazine

Medium: Oil, acrylic on Strathmore board

Size: 10" x 10"

28

Artist: **Jack Unruh**

Art Director: Jill Armus

Client: Saveur

Medium: Ink, watercolor on board

Size: 15" x 14"

29

Artist: **Jack Unruh**

Art Director: Jill Armus

Client: Saveur

Medium: Ink, watercolor on board

Size: 15" x 14"

30

Artist: **Phillip A. Singer**

Art Director: Christine Dunleavy

Client: Philadelphia Inquirer

Medium: Oil on board

Size: 11" x 9"

31

Artist: **Rob Day**

Art Director: Greg Breeding

Client: Journey Communications

Medium: Oil on paper

Size: 14" x 10"

26

27

28

29

30

31

32

Artist: **Tom Curry**
Art Director: Susan Syrnick
Client: Philadelphia Inquirer
Medium: Acrylic on board
Size: 15" x 12"

33

Artist: **Deborah Chabrian**
Medium: Watercolor on paper
Size: 16" x 21"

34

Artist: **Phil Boatwright**
Art Directors: Michael Mrak, Rockwell Harwood
Client: Esquire Magazine
Medium: Oil, acrylic on Strathmore boards
Size: 15" x 12"

35

Artist: **Bill Mayer**
Art Director: Lance Hidy
Client: Harvard Business Review
Medium: Dr. Martin dyes, airbrush on board
Size: 12" x 10"

36

Artist: **Will Terry**
Art Director: Vicki Nightingale
Client: Natural Way
Medium: Acrylic on paper
Size: 14" x 18"

37

Artist: **Etienne Delessert**
Art Director: Marie-Agnes Gaudrat
Client: Pomme D'Api Magazine
Medium: Watercolor on paper

32

33

34

35

36

37

38

Artist: **Gennady Spirin**

Art Director: Lawrence A. Laukhuf

Client: Guideposts

Medium: Watercolor on board

Size: 10" x 8"

39

Artist: **Robert J. Byrd**

Art Director: Ron McCutchan

Client: Spider Magazine

Medium: Ink, colored ink, watercolor on
Arches watercolor paper

Size: 12" x 10"

40

Artist: **Leslie Wu**

Art Director: Gary Kelley

Client: North American Review

Medium: Pastel on paper

Size:: 7" x 6"

41

Artist: **Michael Gibbs**

Art Director: Chris Gibbons

Client: RG Magazine

Medium: Acrylic on board. Artwork
scanned and altered, enhanced in
Photoshop (digital)

Size: 14" x 11"

42

Artist: **Stacy Innerst**

Art Director: Stacy Innerst

Client: Pittsburgh-Post Gazette

Medium: Acrylic on board

Size: 12" x 11"

43

Artist: **Joe Sorren**

Art Director: Jaime Muehlhausen

Client: Snowboarder Magazine

Medium: Acrylic on canvas

Siz:e: 35" x 35""

38

39

40

4I

42

43

44

Artist: **Jeffrey Terreson**

Art Director: Lawrence A. Laukhuf

Client: Guideposts

Medium: Oil on board

Size: 15" x 22"

45

Artist: **Richard Sparks**

Art Director: Joseph P. Connolly

Client: Boys' Life

Medium: Watercolor on board

Size: 22" x 15"

46

Artist: **Bart Forbes**

Art Director: Joseph P. Connolly

Client: Boys' Life

Medium: Oil on canvas

Size: 20" x 20"

47

Artist: **James McMullan**

Art Director: John Boyer

Client: GQ

Medium: Gouache on paper

Size: 11" x 8"

48

Artist: **Kent William**

Art Director: Tom Staebler

Client: Playboy

Medium: Mixed

44

45

46

47

48

49

Artist: **Mike Benny**

Art Director: D.J. Stout

Client: Texas Monthly

Medium: Acrylic

Size: 20" x 23"

50

Artist: **Patrick Arrasmith**

Art Director: Jef Capaldi

Client: American Medical News

Medium: Scratchboard

Size: 13" x 15"

51

Artist: **Patrick Arrasmith**

Art Director: Jef Capaldi

Client: American Medical News

Medium: Scratchboard

Size: 9" x 10"

52

Artist: **John Collier**

Art Director: Andrea Weinstock

Client: The New York Times Magazine

Medium: Monoprint on acetate

Size: 18" x 22"

49

50

51

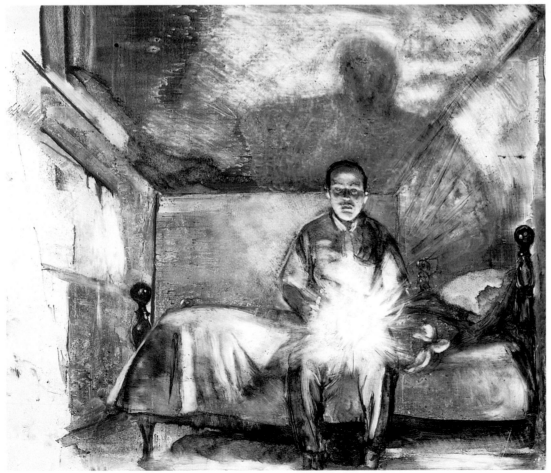

52

54

Artist: **Bernie Fuchs**

Art Director: Charlotte Peterson

Client: Wall St. Journal

Medium: Oil on canvas

Size: 8" x 22"

55

Artist: **Bart Forbes**

Art Director: Joseph P. Connolly

Client: Boys' Life

Medium: Oil on canvas

Size: 23" x 17"

56

Artist: **John Rutkowski**

Art Director: Kim Reister

Client: Houston Alumline Magazine

Medium: Oil

Size: 13" x 11"

57

Artist: **C.F. Payne**

Art Director: Marc Smirnoff

Client: Oxford American

Medium: Mixed on board

Size: 12" x 9"

58

Artist: **Bart Forbes**

Art Director: Joseph P. Connolly

Client: Boys' Life

Medium: Oil on canvas

Size: 12" x 17"

54

55

56

57

58

59

Artist: **C.F. Payne**

Art Director: Fred Woodward

Client: Rolling Stone

Medium: Mixed on board

Size: 16" x 10"

60

Artist: **Stacy Innerst**

Art Director: Stacy Innerst

Client: Pittsburgh-Post Gazette

Medium: Acrylic on board

Size: 12" x 9"

61

Artist: **Joseph Lorusso**

Art Director: Phil Bratter

Client: Worth Magazine

Medium: Oil on board

Size: 12" x 9"

62

Artist: **Steve Brodner**

Art Director: Eric Baker

Client: Public The New Republic

Medium: Watercolor, pastel on paper

Size: 15" x 13"

63

Artist: **Mark Summers**

Art Director: Steve Heller

Client: The New York Times Book Review

Medium: Scratchboard

Size: 7" x 5"

64

Artist: **Mark Summers**

Art Director: Steve Heller

Client: The New York Times Book Review

Medium: Scratchboard

Size: 6" x 5"

59

60

61

62

63

64

65

Artist: **Daniel Adel**

Art Director: David Matt

Client: Premiere Magazine

Medium: Oil on panel

Size: 24" x 29"

66

Artist: **Gary Kelley**

Art Directors: Alisha Drucks, John Korpics

Client: Entertainment Weekly

Medium: Pastel on paper

Size: 15" x 13"

67

Artist: **Anita Kunz**

Art Director: Joe Kimberling

Client: Entertainment Weekly

Medium: Watercolor, gouache on board

Size: 11" x 9"

68

Artist: **Phil Boatwright**

Art Director: Stephanie Finks

Client: POV Magazine

Medium: Oil, acrylic, collage on Strathmore board

Size: 11" x 8"

69

Artist: **Marco Ventura**

Art Directors: Tom Staebler, Kerig Pope

Client: Playboy

Medium: Oil on paper

Size: 12" x 9"

70

Artist: **Daniel Adel**

Art Director: George McCalman

Client: Entertainment Weekly

Medium: Oil on panel

Size: 15" x 11"

65

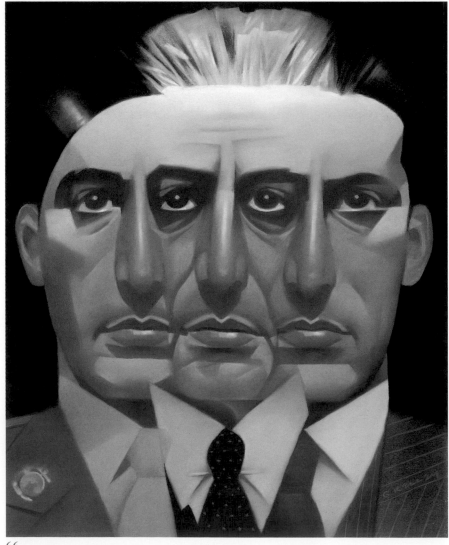

66

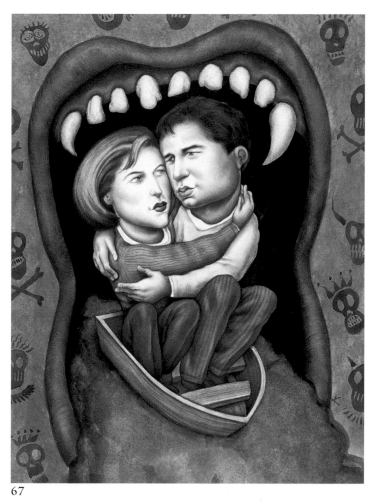

67

68

69

70

71

Artist: **Tim Bower**

Art Director: Geraldine Hessler

Client: Rolling Stone

Medium: Gouache on board

Size: 10" x 6"

72

Artist: **Steve Brodner**

Art Director: Kerry Tremain

Client: Mother Jones Magazine

Medium: Watercolor, pastel on paper

Size: 14" x 9"

73

Artist: **C.F. Payne**

Art Directors: Arthur Hochstein,
                 Kenneth Smith

Client: Time

Medium: Mixed on board

Size: 9" x 8"

74

Artist: **Harry F. Bliss**

Art Directors: Frank Baseman, Betsy Brecht

Client: Philadelphia Magazine

Medium: Watercolor on Arches
          watercolor paper

Size: 13" x 9"

75

Artist: **Gary Aagaard**

Medium: Oil on canvas

Size: 36" X 24"

72

73

74

75

76

Artist: **Michelle Barnes**

Art Director: Nicki Kalish

Client: The New York Times Magazine/
The Sophisticated Traveler

Medium: Acrylic on board

Size: 18" x 13"

77

Artist: **John English**

Art Director: Christine Morrison

Client: Stocks & Commodities

Medium: Oil on canvas

78

Artist: **Will Terry**

Art Director: Vicky Snow

Client: Arizona Highways

Medium: Acrylic on paper

Size: 15" x 15"

79

Artist: **Gregory Manchess**

Art Director: Bob Goodfellow

Client: Fine Woodworking Magazine

Medium: Oil on linen

Size: 17" x 12"

80

Artist: **Janet Woolley**

Art Director: Eugene Wang

Client: Unlimited Magazine

Medium: Mixed on board

Size: 12" x 22"

76

77

78

79

80

81

Artist: **Sam Ward**

Art Director: Duane Flinchum

Agency: Finchum Inc.

Client: Reform Judaism Magazine

Medium: Gouache on Bristol

Size: 17" x 24"

82

Artist: **Tim Borgert**

Art Director: Lee Waigand

Client: Dayton Daily News

Medium: Mixed on board

Size: 9" x 18"

83

Artist: **Raúl Colón**

Art Director: Ken McFarlin

Client: The New York Times Magazine/
The Sophisticated Traveler

Medium: Watercolor, colored pencil on
watercolor paper

Size: 17" x 14"

84

Artist: **Raúl Colón**

Art Director: Stephanie Phelan

Client: Women's Day

Medium: Watercolor, colored pencil on
watercolor paper

Size: 17" x 13"

85

Artist: **Robert Rodriguez**

Art Director: Lawrence A. Laukhuf

Client: Guideposts

Medium: Oil on wood

Size: 15" x 20"

81

82

83

84

85

86
Artist: **Jody Hewgill**
Art Director: Cynthia Friedman
Client: Modern Maturity
Medium: Acrylic on board
Size: 13" x 10"

87
Artist: **Jody Hewgill**
Art Director: George Karabotsos
Client: Out Magazine
Medium: Acrylic on board
Size: 9 1/2" x 10"

88
Artist: **Jody Williams**
Medium: Oil on paper
Size: 9" x 9"

89
Artist: **John Collier**
Art Director: Margot Frankel
Client: Town & Country
Medium: Monoprint on acetate
Size: 12" x 10"

90
Artist: **Tim Jessell**
Art Director: Jeanne Devlin
Client: Oklahoma Today Magazine
Medium: Pastel, mixed on paper
Size: 15" x 11"

91
Artist: **Tim Jessell**
Art Director: Jeanne Devlin
Client: Oklahoma Today Magazine
Medium: Monoprint on acetate
Size: 15" x 15"

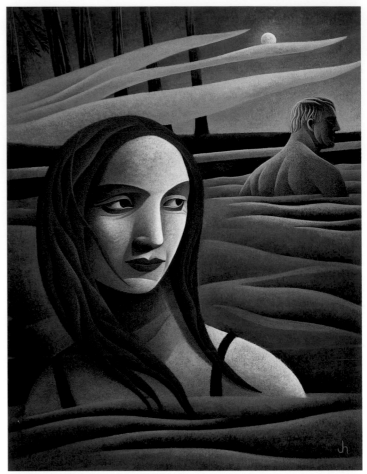

86

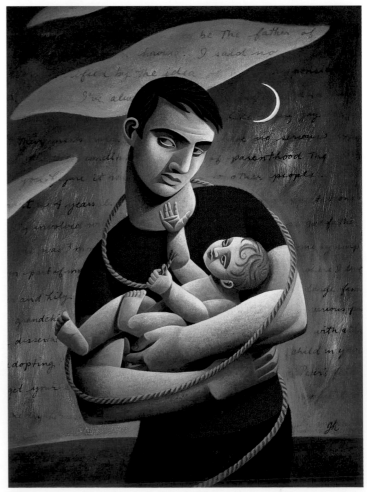

87

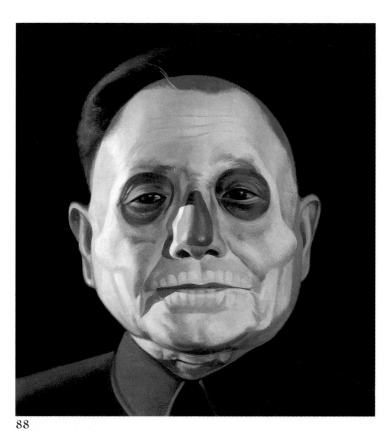

88

89

90

91

92

Artist: **Donato Giancola**

Art Director: Kerig Pope

Client: Playboy

Medium: Oil, acrylic on paper mounted
    on masonite

Size: 21" x 25"

93

Artist: **Michael Gibbs**

Art Director: Steve Scheiner

Client: Bellcore Exchange

Medium: Acrylic on board. Artwork
    scanned and altered, enhanced
    in Photoshop (digital)

Size: 14" x 10"

94

Artist: **Ingo Fast**

Art Director: Kevin Dresser

Client: Flatiron News

Medium: Pen & ink, watercolor, color
    pencil on watercolor paper

Size: 14" x11"

95

Artist: **Steven Guarnaccia**

Art Director: Robert Jensen

Client: Design Quarterly

Medium: Pen & ink, watercolor on watercolor
    paper

Size:: 14" x 11"

96

Artist: **Earl Keleny**

Art Director: KristinFitzpatrick

Client: Chicago Tribune

Medium: Watercolor on paper

Size: 11" x 11"

92

93

94

95

96

97

Artist: **Peter de Sève**
Art Director: Chris Curry
Client: The New Yorker
Medium: Watercolor, ink on watercolor paper
Size: 12" x 9"

98

Artist: **Gregory Manchess**
Art Director: John Boyer
Client: GQ
Medium: Oil
Size: 26" x 19""

99

Artist: **John Thompson**
Art Directors: Tom Staebler, Kerig Pope
Client: Playboy
Medium: Acrylic on Crescent #1 board
Size: 16" x 16"

100

Artist: **Francis Livingston**
Client: Nob Hill Gazette
Medium: Oil on board
Size: 12" x 11"

101

Artist: **Gary Kelley**
Art Directors: Tom Staebler, Kerig Pope
Client: Playboy
Medium: Pastel on paper
Size: 21" x 19"

97

98

99

100

101

102

Artist: **Istvan Banyai**
Art Director: Tom Staebler
Client: Playboy
Medium: Digital

103

Artist: **Guy Billout**
Art Director: Judy Garlan
Client: The Atlantic Monthly
Medium: Watercolor on Bristol vellum
Size: 10" x 8"

104

Artist: **Guy Billout**
Art Director: Judy Garlan
Client: The Atlantic Monthly
Medium: Watercolor on Bristol vellum
Size: 10" x 7"

105

Artist: **Richard Sparks**
Art Director: Joseph P. Connolly
Client: Boys' Life
Medium: Watercolor on board
Size: 23" x 17"

106

Artist: **Robert G. Steele**
Art Director: Mary Ellis
Client: Our State Magazine
Medium: Watercolor on paper
Size: 14" x 21"

102

103

104

105

106

BOOK JURY

Jerry Pinkney
Chairman, Illustrator

Jerry Demoney
Design Director, Mobil Corporation

Gail P. Dubov
Associate Art Director, Avon Books

John Ennis
Illustrator

Judy Francis
Illustrator

Victor Gadino
Illustrator, Portrait artist

Irene Gallo
Art Director, Tor/Forge Books

Eugene Hoffman
Illustrator/Professor, University of Northern Colorado

Martha Vaughan
Illustrator

BOOK

AWARD WINNERS

GREGORY MANCHESS
Gold Medal

DEAN MORRISSEY
Gold Medal

JOHN THOMPSON
Gold Medal

BOB DACEY
Silver Medal

IRENE HAAS
Silver Medal

STEPHEN T. JOHNSON
Silver Medal

112

Artist: **Gregory Manchess**

Art Director: Nancy Leo

Client: Dial Books for Young Readers

Medium: Oil on canvas

Size: 25" x 40"

"I love the guts and decisiveness that many illustrators often pour into their pictures with copious abandon. When Dial Books called with a Celtic myth, *To Capture the Wind*, by Sheila MacGill-Callahan, it was begging for that kind of focus and I was happy to dive in. It got even better when I discovered that it had a strong feminine hero who didn't take 'no' for an answer. I let my classic influences take over and started laying on the paint. Sheer joy. Of course, taking a Gold from the Society was just the right touch."

113

Artist: **Dean Morrissey**

Art Director: Robert Morton

Client: Harry N. Abrams Inc.

Medium: Oil on linen

Size:: 20" x 59"

"I've been drawing most of my life and being recognized by the Society is the greatest honor of my career. I see no distinction between illustration and fine art. To me, there is only inspired work and uninspired work, the latter being mediocre by definition—I have done both and know the difference. Sometimes, but not always, during the making of a painting the picture takes hold of you. The sensation is that you are hanging onto the brushes for the ride. When that happens, you feel completely artistically alive. That's what I'm looking for every time I stretch a canvas."

114

Artist: **John Thompson**

Art Director: Elizabeth B. Parisi

Client: Scholastic Inc.

Medium: Acrylic on ragboard

Size: 23" x 14"

"Born in Three Rivers, Michigan, and raised in South Bend, Indiana, life as an artist began at an early age. My father was an artist and my brother and I had great stuff to play with while we were growing up.

"'True North' is part of a series of paintings I have done dealing with the lives and history of African-Americans. I feel fortunate that I have had the opportunity to contribute my vision to the words I have been given."

115

Artist: **Bob Dacey**

Art Director: David Saylor

Client: Scholastic Inc.

Medium: Watercolor on Strathmore

Size: 14" x 23"

"This scene from the book *Miriam's Cup* depicts one of the plagues sent down on the Egyptians in the Exodus story. The book focuses on Miriam, Moses' older sister, and the importance of her role in Exodus. There is a rapidly growing movement to have Miriam recognized by including a cup of water in her honor during the Seder. My partner, Debra Bandelin, and I spent an intense three months researching, gathering reference, and producing the 16 paintings for this book."

116

Artist: **Irene Haas**

Art Director: Ann Bobco

Client: Simon & Schuster Books for
Young Readers

Medium: Watercolor, pastel on paper

Size: 10" x 23"

"This picture is the big party scene from my book *A Summertime Song*. In it, everyone from the garden is dancing the night away underneath the flowers and the plants. I think it is the illustration which best describes the premise of the story—that magic sometimes happens. *A Summertime Song* is the third book I've written after more than 40 years of illustrating picture books written by others. I don't enjoy writing and it takes me forever, but it's what I do in order to paint the images I love. Getting a medal from the Society of Illustrators certainly confirms my book's premise that magic sometimes happens!"

117

Artist: **Stephen T. Johnson**

Art Directors: Michael Farmer, Stephen T. Johnson, Kaelin Chappell

Client: Harcourt Brace & Co.

Medium: Pastel on paper

Size: 18" x 24"

"I would like to credit my editor Paula Wiseman at Harcourt Brace/Silver Whistle for her help and encouragement and for giving me complete freedom to pursue my vision for the book *Hoops*. I always welcome an inspiring project and *Hoops* was the impetus to push my art in a different and exciting direction. I think the art captures the poetry of the text and the energy of the game. An unfinished quality to the illustrations, I hope, conveys a contemporary yet classical feeling."

118

Artist: **Gary Kelley**

Art Director: Atha Tehon

Client: Dial Books for Young Readers

Medium: Pastel on paper

Size: 17" x 13"

119

Artist: **Gregory Manchess**

Art Director: Nancy Leo

Client: Dial Books for Young Readers

Medium: Oil on canvas

Size: 25" x 40"

120

Artist: **David Shannon**

Art Director: Atha Tehon

Client: Dial Books for Young Readers

Medium: Acrylic on board

Size: 13" x 21"

121

Artist: **Charles Santore**

Art Director: Cathy Goldsmith

Client: Random House

Medium: Watercolor on Arches

Size: 11" x 17"

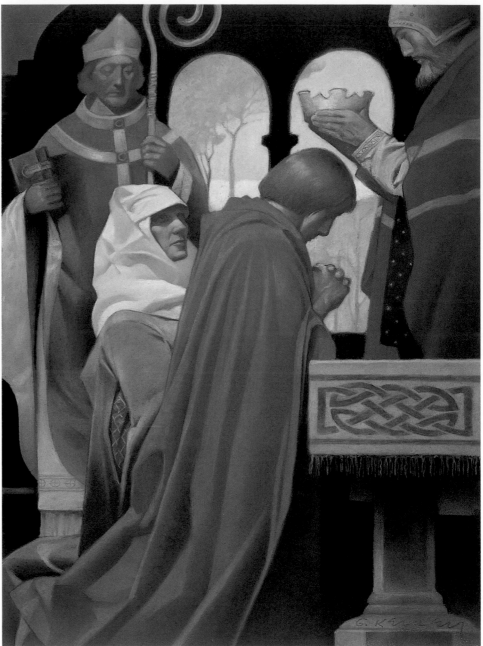

118

119

122

Artist: **Duane O. Myers**

Art Director: Judith Murello

Client: Putnam Berkley Publishing Group

Medium: Oil on masonite

Size: 28" x 17"

123

Artist: **Charles Santore**

Art Director: Cathy Goldsmith

Client: Random House

Medium: Watercolor on Arches

Size: 12" x 18"

124

Artist: **Don Maitz**

Art Director: Jane Johnson

Client: HarperCollins

Medium: Oil on masonite

Size: 22" x 29"

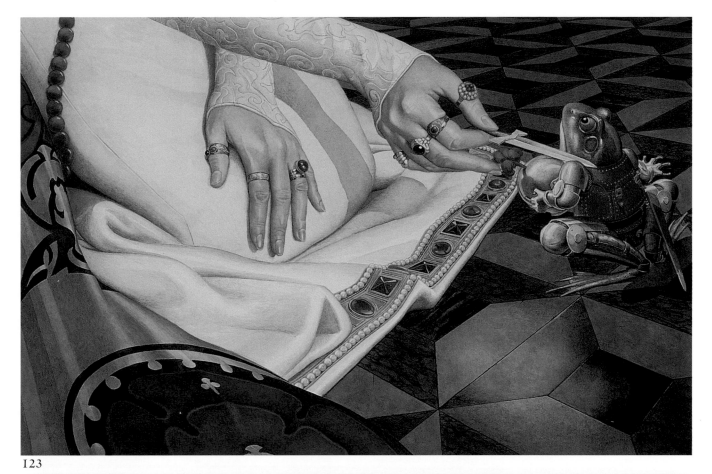

123

124

125

Artist: **John Ennis**

Art Director: Sophia Duffy

Client: Zebra Books

Medium: Digital, Photoshop, Bryce

Size: 14" x 9"

126

Artist: **John Ennis**

Art Director: Gene Mydlowski

Client: HarperCollins

Medium: Digital, Photoshop, Bryce, Painter

Size: 12" x 18"

127

Artist: **Kinuko Craft**

Art Director: Roseanne J. Serra

Client: Penguin USA

Medium: Mixed on board

Size: 22" x 13"

128

Artist: **David Bowers**

Art Director: Kristen M. Nobles

Client: St. Martin's Press

Medium: Oil on masonite

Size: 19" x 12"

125

126

127

128

129

Artist: **Tristan Elwell**

Art Director: Tom Egner

Client: Avon Books

Medium: Oil on masonite

Size" 15" x 9"

130

Artist: **Rob Day**

Art Director: Tom Stvan

Client: Free Press

Medium: Oil on paper

Size: 13" x 24"

131

Artist: **Bob Dacey**

Art Director: David Saylor

Client: Scholastic Inc.

Medium: Watercolor on Strathmore

Size: 14" x 23"

132

Artist: **John Thompson**

Art Director: Barbara Fitzsimmons

Agency: Goodhue & Assoc.

Client: Morrow Junior Books

Medium: Acrylic on Bristol

Size: 15" x 12"

129

130

131

132

133

Artist: **Tristan Elwell**

Art Director: Lisa Peters

Client: Harcourt Brace & Co.

Medium: Oil on masonite

Size: 17" x 11"

134

Artist: **Rafal Olbinski**

Art Director: Elene Jacob

Client: Golden Books

Medium: Acrylic on linen

Size: 30" x 20"

135

Artist: **Jean Cassels**

Art Directors: Jean Cassels, Paige Gillies

Medium: Gouache

Size: 10" x 7"

136

Artist: **John Jude Palencar**

Art Director: Judith Murello

Client: Putnam Berkley Publishing Group

Medium: Oil

Size: 9" x 10"

137

Artist: **Christian Birmingham**

Art Director: Ian Butterworth

Medium: Pastel on paper

Size: 16" x 12"

133

134

135

136

137

138

Artist: **Bill Sienkiewicz**
Art Director: Robin Brosterman
Client: D.C. Comics
Medium: Watercolor on board
Size: 15" x 10"

139

Artist: **David Shannon**
Art Director: Atha Tehon
Client: Dial Books for Young Readers
Medium: Acrylic on board
Size: 13" x 21"

140

Artist: **Timothy Basil Ering**
Art Director: Lynette Ruschak
Client: DK Ink
Medium: Mixed on paper
Size: 11" x 8"

141

Artist: **Murray Tinkelman**
Art Director: Vincent DiFate
Client: Viking/Penguin
Medium: Pen & ink, dyes on Bristol
Size: 17" x 12"

139

140

141

142

Artist: **Kazuhiko Sano**

Art Director: Sachiko Sakurai

Client: Shincho-sha Publishing

Medium: Acrylic, mixed on masonite

Size: 24" x 17"

143

Artist: **Yuri Bartoli**

Medium: Oil on board

Size: 12" x 14"

144

Artist: **Yuri Bartoli**

Medium: Oil on masonite

Size: 43" x 33"

145

Artist: **Tim O'Brien**

Art Directors: Tom Egner, Gail Dubov

Client: Avon Books

Medium: Oil on board

Size: 14" x 9"

146

Artist: **John Jude Palencar**

Art Director: John Fontana

Client: Scribner Books

Medium: Acrylic on ragboard

Size: 15" x 18"

142

143

144

145

146

147

Artist: **Marvin Mattelson**

Art Director: Lorraine Paradowski

Client: Scholastic Inc.

Medium: Mixed on paper

Size: 15" x 11"

148

Artist: **Teresa Fasolino**

Art Director: Joni Friedman

Client: Putnam Berkley Publishing Group

Medium: Oil on canvas

Size: 18" x 13"

149

Artist: **Douglas Fraser**

Art Directors: Jackie Meyer, Rachel McClain

Client: Warner Books

Medium: Alkyds (oil base) on canvas

Size: 11" x 9"

150

Artist: **Chris Gall**

Art Directors: Julia Kushnirsky, Rachel McClain

Client: Warner Books

Medium: Pen & ink, waterxoloe on Arches

Size: 14" x 9"

151

Artist: **Michael Dudash**

Art Director: Clair Moritz

Client: Reader's Digest Condensed Books

Medium: Oil on linen mounted on gator foam

Size:: 16" x 22"

147

148

149

150

151

152

Artist: **Michael Dudash**

Art Director: Clair Moritz

Client: Reader's Digest Condensed Books

Medium: Oil on linen mounted on gator foam

Size: 16" x 22"

153

Artist: **Michael Dudash**

Art Director: Clair Moritz

Client: Reader's Digest Condensed Books

Medium: Oil on linen mounted on gator foam

Size: 18" x 13"

154

Artist: **Jeff Barson**

Art Director: Judith Murello

Client: Putnam Berkley Publishing Group

Medium: Oil on board

155

Artist: **Bart Forbes**

Art Director: Lisa Chovnick

Client: Macmillan Publishing Co.

Medium: Oil on canvas

Size: 19" x 29"

152

153

154

155

156

Artist: **Jerry Pinkney**

Art Director: Claire Couniham

Client: Scholastic Inc.

Medium: Pencil, watercolor on paper

Size: 17" x 13"

157

Artist: **Craig Tennant**

Medium: Oil on canvas

158

Artist: **Craig Tennant**

Medium: Oil on canvas

156

157

158

159

Artist: **Jerry Pinkney**

Art Director: Atha Tehon

Client: Dial Books for Young Readers

Medium: Pencil, watercolor on Arches watercolor paper

Size: 15" x 22"

160

Artist: **John Suh**

Medium: Oil on canvas

Size: 10" x 16"

161

Artist: **Dean Morrissey**

Art Director: Robert Morton

Client: Harry N. Abrams Inc.

Medium: Oil on linen

Size: 20" x 47"

162

Artist: **Dean Morrissey**

Art Director: Robert Morton

Client: Harry N. Abrams Inc.

Medium: Oil on linen

Size: 24" x 35"

159

160

161

162

163

Artist: **John Craig**

Art Director: Simms Taback

Client: Graphic Artists Guild

Medium: Collage, digital

Size: 15" x 9"

164

Artist: **Albert Lorenz**

Art Directors: Darilyn Lowe Carnes,
 Joy Schleh

Client: Harry N. Abrams, Inc.

Medium: Mixed on Bristol

Size: 28" x 19"

165

Artist: **Albert Lorenz**

Art Directors: Darilyn Lowe Carnes,
 Joy Schleh

Client: Harry N. Abrams, Inc.

Medium: Mixed on Bristol

Size: 19" x 14"

166

Artist: **Bob Crofut**

Medium: Oil on canvas

167

Artist: **Michael Whelan**

Medium: Acrylic on watercolor board

Size: 11" x 12"

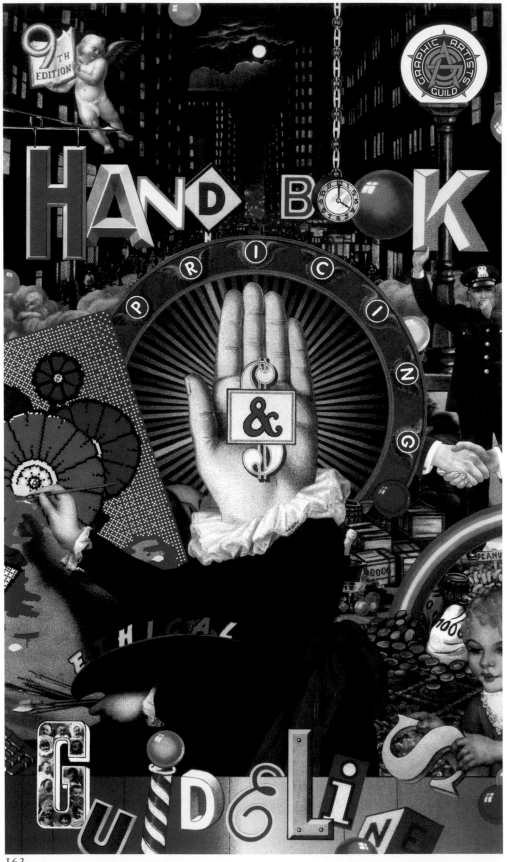

163

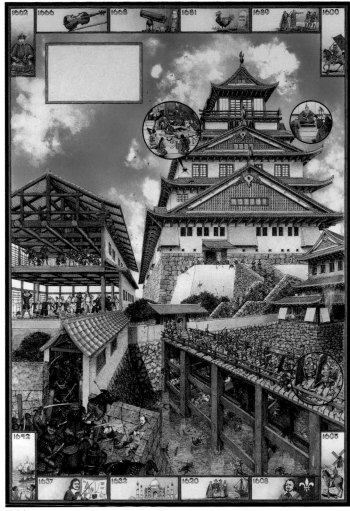

164

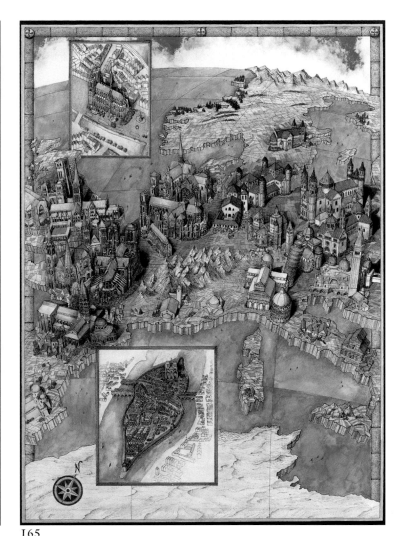

165

166

167

168

Artist: **Joanie Schwarz**

Art Director: Georgia Morrissey

Client: Random House

Medium: Digital, Photoshop/Painter

Size: 10" x 7"

169

Artist: **Tom Pohrt**

Art Director: Barbara Ras

Client: University of Georgia Press

Medium: Watercolor on paper

Size: 4" x 6"

170

Artist: **S. Saelig Gallagher**

Art Director: Elizabeth B. Parisi

Client: Scholastic Inc.

Medium: Mixed on paper

Size: 15" x 11"

171

Artist: **Wayne Alfano**

Art Director: Gail Dubov

Client: Avon Books

Medium: Oil on gessoed masonite

Size: 34" x 22"

172

Artist: **Lori McElrath-Eslick**

Art Director: Tim Gilner

Client: Boyds Mills Press

Medium Oil on masonite

Size: 7" x 5"

173

Artist: **John Collier**

Art Director: John Kelly

Client: Barnes & Noble, Inc.

Medium Pastel, watercolor on paper

Size: 23" x 18"

168

169

170

171

172

173

174

Artist: **Ken Hamilton**
Medium: Oil on linen
Size: 23" x 17"

175

Artist: **John Suh**
Client: Saks Gallery
Medium: Oil on canvas
Size: 15" x 20"

176

Artist: **Kam Mak**
Art Director: Al Cetta
Client: HarperCollins
Medium: Oil on panel
Size: 13" x 20"

177

Artist: **Brian Pinkney**
Art Director: Mara Van Fleet
Client: Hyperion Books
Medium: Mixed, scratchboard
Size: 11" x 17"

174

175

176

177

178

Artist: **Brian Pinkney**

Art Director: Mara Van Fleet

Client: Hyperion Books

Medium: Mixed, scratchboard

Size: 11" x 17"

179

Artist: **Brian Pinkney**

Art Director: Mara Van Fleet

Client: Hyperion Books

Medium: Mixed, scratchboard

Size: 11" x 17"

180

Artist: **Stephen T. Johnson**

Art Directors: Michael Farmer, Stephen T. Johnson, Kaelin Chappell

Client: Harcourt Brace & Co.

Medium: Pastel on paper

Size: 24" x 18"

181

Artist: **Stephen T. Johnson**

Art Directors: Michael Farmer, Stephen T. Johnson, Kaelin Chappell

Client: Harcourt Brace & Co.

Medium: Pastel on paper

Size: 20" x16"

182

Artist: **Cathleen Toelke**

Art Director: John Candell

Client: Henry Holt & Co.

Medium: Pastel on paper

Size: 15" x18"

178

179

180

181

182

183

Artist: **Wilson McLean**

Art Director: Cherlynne C. Li

Client: Simon & Schuster

Medium: Oil on canvas

Size: 15" x 11"

184

Artist: Franco Accornero

Art Director: Janice Rossi

Client: Kensington Publishing

Medium: Digital

Size: 21" x 20"

185

Artist: **Herb Tauss**

Art Directors: Julie Rauer, Atha Tehon

Client: Dial Books for Young Readers

Medium: Charcoal, oil crayon on canvas

Size: 15" x 10"

186

Artist: **Michael Koelsch**

Art Director: Irene Gallo

Client: Tor Books

Medium: Digital

Size: 35" x 23"

183

184

185

186

187

Artist: **John Thompson**

Art Director: Kathleen Westray

Client: Scholastic Inc.

Medium: Acrylic on Bristol

Size: 10" x 8"

188

Artist: **John Thompson**

Art Director: Kathleen Westray

Client: Scholastic Inc.

Medium: Acrylic on Bristol

Size: 10" x 8"

189

Artist: **Etienne Delessert**

Art Director: Rita Marshall

Client: Gallimard Publishing

Medium: Acrylic on wood

Size: 24" x 17"

190

Artist: **Etienne Delessert**

Art Director: Rita Marshall

Client: Gallimard Publishing

Medium: Acrylic on wood

191

Artist: **Etienne Delessert**

Art Director: Rita Marshall

Client: Gallimard Publishing

Medium: Acrylic on wood

Size: 24" x 18"

187

188

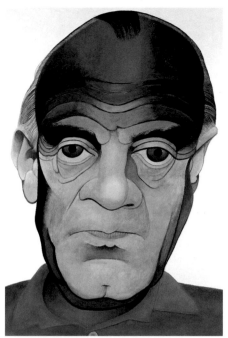

189

190

191

192

Artist: **Ralph Butler**
Art Director: Howard Grossman
Client: John Wiley & Sons
Medium: Acrylic on laurel wood panel
Size: 16" x 11"

193

Artist: **Jim Burke**
Art Directors: John English, Mark English
Medium: Mixed on board
Size: 13" x 10"

194

Artist: **Hiro Kimura**
Medium: Mixed
Size: 16" x 10"

195

Artist: **Kam Mak**
Art Director: Al Cetta
Client: HarperCollins
Medium: Oil on panel
Size: 16" x 13"

192

193

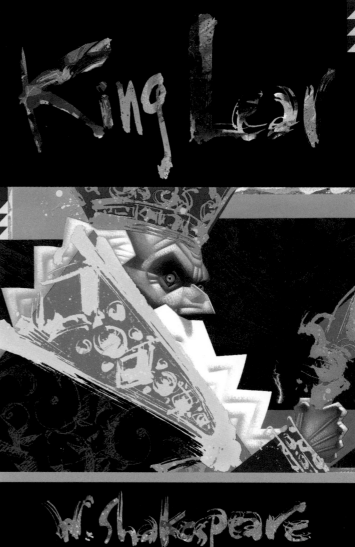

194

195

196

Artist: **John Jude Palencar**

Art Director: Judith Murello

Client: Putnam Berkley Publishing Group

Medium: Acrylic on ragboard

Size: 25" x 26"

197

Artist: **Phil Boatwright**

Art Directors: David Uttley, Diane Weisner

Client: Honor Books

Medium: Oil, acrylic on Strathmore board

Size: 14" x13"

198

Artist: **Leonid Gore**

Art Directors: Anne Bobco, Angela Carlino

Client: Simon & Schuster Books for
Young Readers

Medium: Acrylic on paper

Size: 12" x 9"

199

Artist: **Bruce Jensen**

Art Director: Judith Murello

Client: Putnam Berkley Publishing Group

Medium: Acrylic on board

Size: 23" x 16"

200

Artist: **Bernie Fuchs**

Art Director: Atha Tehon

*Client:*Dial Books for Young Readers

Medium: Pencil, oil on paper

Size: 24" x 38"

196

197

198

199

200

201

Artist: **Troy Howell**
Art Director: Dianne Hess
Client: Scholastic Inc.
Medium: Acrylic on ragboard
Size: 14" x 10"

202

Artist: **Marni Backer**
Art Director: Jessica Kirchoff
Client: Turtle Books
Medium: Oil on Bristol paper
Size: 15" x 15"

203

Artist: **David Christiana**
Art Director: Dee Timba
Client: Harcourt Brace & Co.
Medium: Watercolor on paper
Size: 8" x 20"

204

Artists: **Steve Johnson, Lou Fancher**
Art Directors: Denise Cronin, Lou Fancher
Client: Viking/Penguin
Medium: Acrylic on masonite

201

202

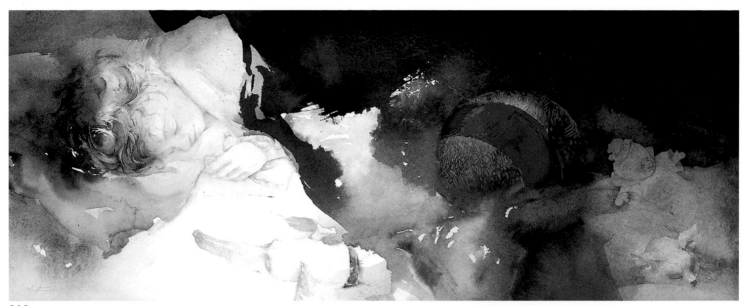

203

204

205

Artist: **Jos A. Smith**

Art Director: Ava Weiss

Client: Greenwillow Books

Medium: Watercolor on Arches
watercolor paper

Size: 14" x 24"

206

Artist: **David Shannon**

Art Director: Elizabeth B. Parisi

Client: Scholastic Inc.

Medium: Acrylic on board

Size: 11" x 8"

207

Artist: **Tom Curry**

Art Director: Melanie Kroupa

Client: Orchard Books

Medium: Acrylic on board

Size: 10" x 18"

208

Artist: **John Nickle**

Art Director: Ann Bobco

Client: Atheneum Books

Medium: Acrylic on watercolor paper

Size: 9" x 11"

205

206

207

209

Artist: **John Ward**

Art Director: Ann Stott

Client: Candlewick Press

Medium: Acrylic on canvas

Size: 9" x 13"

210

Artist: **Ellen Thompson**

Art Director: Gail Dubov

Client: Avon Books

Medium: Watercolor on Strathmore Bristol

Size: 13" x 9"

211

Artist: **Brad Sneed**

Art Director: Bob Kosturko

Client: Houghton Mifflin Co.

Medium: Watercolor on watercolor paper

Size: 14" x 10"

212

Artist: **Michael Koelsch**

Art Director: Vaughn Andrews

Client: Harcourt Brace & Co.

Medium: Acrylic on board

Size: 15" x 10"

213

Artist: **Lydia Thompson**

Art Director: Alex Bostic

Agency: Illumination Studio

Client: Sights Productions

Medium: Mixed on paper

Size: 21" x 19"

214

Artist: **Christopher Wormell**

Art Director: Ian Butterworth

Client: Clarkson Potter

Medium: Linocut on paper

Size: 10" x 7"

209

210

211

212

213

214

215

Artist: **Dennis Ziemienski**

Art Director: John Fontana

Client: Scribner

Medium: Acrylic on 100% rag

216

Artist: **Wendell Minor**

Art Director: Linda Zuckerman

Client: Harcourt Brace & Co./
Browndeer Press

Medium: Watercolor on cold press paper

Size: 9" x 9"

217

Artist: **Tom Curry**

Art Director: Melanie Kroupa

Client: Orchard Books

Medium: Acrylic on hardboard

Size: 10" x 11"

218

Artist: **Kam Mak**

Art Director: Julia Kushnirsky

Client: St. Martin's Press

Medium: Oil on panel

Size: 16" x 12"

215

216

218

217

219

Artist: **Mark Hess**
Art Director: Sheila Gilbert
Client: Daw Books
Medium: Acrylic, oil on canvas
Size: 15" x 10"

220

Artist: **Bruce Garrity**
Art Director: Kathy Kuhl
Client: Philadelphia Creative Directory
Medium: Oil, alkyd on masonite
Size: 11" x 8"

221

Artist: **Julian Allen**
Art Director: Krystyna Skalsi
Client: Walker & Co.
Medium: Watercolor on paper
Size: 15" x 10"

222

Artist: **Carol Schwartz**
Art Director: Sylvia Frezzolini Severence
Client: Mondo Publishing
Medium: Gouache on Strathmore Bristol
Size: 13" x 22"

223

Artist: **Jonathan Bumas**
Art Director: Jonathan Bumas
Client: Flyleaf Publishing
Medium: Watercolor, pastels on paper
Size: 12" x 14"

219

220

221

222

223

225
Artist: **Charles Santore**
Art Director: Cathy Goldsmith
Client: Random House
Medium: Watercolor on Arches
Size: 12" x 18"

226
Artist: **Mike Russell**
Art Director: Gail Dubov
Client: Avon Books
Medium: Colored pencil on museum board
Size: 12" x 16"

227
Artist: **Tom Pohrt**
Art Director: Barbara Ras
Client: University of Georgia Press
Medium: Watercolor on paper
Size: 6" x 9"

228
Artist: **Wendell Minor**
Art Director: Al Cetta
Client: HarperCollins
Medium: Acrylic on masonite
Size: 13" x 11"

229
Artist: **Wendell Minor**
Art Director: Ellen Friedman
Client: Hyperion Books
Medium: Watercolor on cold press paper
Size: 12" x 18"

225

226

227

228

229

230

Artist: **Jerry LoFaro**

Art Directors: Lori Cohen, Phil Unetic

Client: Time Life Books

Medium: Acrylic, airbrush on board

Size: 13" x 10"

231

Artist: **Christopher Denise**

Art Director: Patrick Collins

Client: Philomel Books

Medium: Pastel, charcoal on paper

Size: 12" x 20"

232

Artist: **Frank Riccio**

Art Director: Frank Riccio

Client: Grace Publishing & Communications

Medium: Oil on watercolor paper

Size: 29" x 23"

233

Artist: **Robin Brickman**

Art Directors: Lucille Chomowicz, Paul Zakris

Client: Simon & Schuster Books
for Young Readers

Medium: Paper, watercolor on paper, glue

Size: 12" x 23"

230

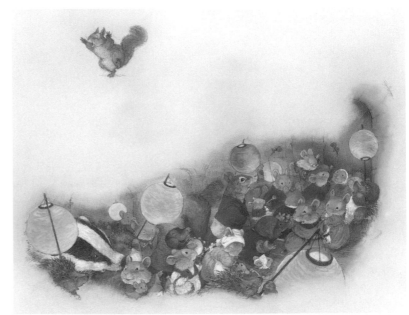

231

232

233

234

Artist: **Bruce Whatley**

Art Director: Tom Starace

Client: HarperCollins

Medium: Watercolor, gouche on
Letramax 2200 board

Size: 13" x 21"

235

Artist: **Don Daily**

Art Director: Paul Kepple

Client: Running Press

Medium: Watercolor on D'Arches
90lb coldpress

Size: 13" x 10"

236

Artist: **Don Daily**

Art Director: Paul Kepple

Client: Running Press

Medium: Watercolor on D'Arches
90lb coldpress

Size: 13" x 19"

237

Artist: **Patrick O'Brien**

Art Director: Martha Rago

Client: Henry Holt & Co.

Medium: Oil on canvas

Size: 20" x 16"

238

Artist: **Ashley Wolff**

Art Director: Al Cetta

Client: HarperCollins

Medium: Gouache on Arches

Size: 11" x 17"

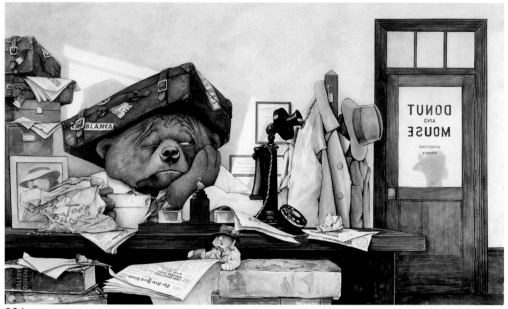

234

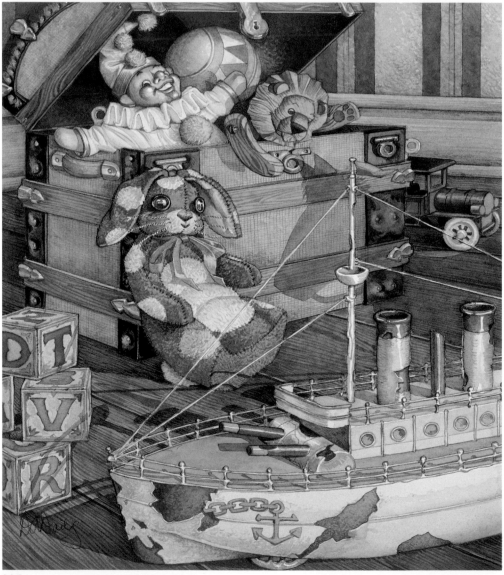

235

236

237

238

243

Artist: **Tim Jessell**

Client: Creative Company

Medium: Pastel, mixed on paper

244

Artist: **Oscar Senn**

Medium: Oil on canvas

245

Artist: **Greg Call**

Art Director: Irene Gallo

Client: Tor Books

Medium: Oil on board

Size: 25" x 16"

246

Artist: **Chris Sheban**

Art Director: Rita Marshall

Client: Creative Education

Medium: Watercolor, Prismacolor
pencil on paper

Size: 10" x 20"

247

Artist: **Chris Sheban**

Art Director: Rita Marshall

Client: Creative Education

Medium: Watercolor, Prismacolor
pencil on paper

Size: 13" x 13"

248

Artist: **Henry Cole**

Art Director: Ellen Friedman

Client: Hyperion Books for Children

Medium: Acrylic, colored pencil on
watercolor paper

Size: 12" x 15"

243

244

245

246

247

248

Joe Ciardiello
Chairman, Illustrator

Joseph P. Connolly
Boy Scouts of America

Richard Egielski
Illustrator

Randall Enos
Illustrator

Gerry Gersten
Illustrator

Anita Kunz
Illustrator

Lawrence A. Laukhuf
Director of Art and Design, Guideposts

Daniel Pelavin
Illustrator

Irena Roman
Illustrator

AWARD
WINNERS

TOM CHRISTOPHER
Silver Medal

ETIENNE DELESSERT
Silver Medal

GRACE DeVITO
Silver Medal

KADIR NELSON
Silver Medal

249

Artist: **Tom Christopher**

Art Director: Peter Schaefer

Client: The New York Times

Size: 40" x 30"

"Pete Schaefer gave me a job to paint something with the New York Times Building in it. As I stood in front of the building watching how quickly the blue/purple shadows from the late summer light move, this messenger kid came gliding down the street sandwiched between two cabs. As he was looking up at the flags, I grabbed this image. It seemed to symbolize a big city aspiration of either working for an important paper or being important enough to have an article written about you. Most likely, it's just a guy trying to find an address, but I like the painting anyway."

250

Artist: **Etienne Delessert**

Art Director: Rita Marshall

Client: Olympic Museum

Medium: Watercolor on paper

Size: 16" x 12"

This piece was used for the poster and catalog cover for a large (150 pieces) retrospective of Delessert's work at the new Olympic Museum in Lausanne, Switzerland. The show will travel to France, Taiwan, New York and Japan.

251

Artist: **Grace DeVito**

Art Director: Susan Lage

Client: Sigma Advertising

Medium: Oil on board

Size: 10" x 11"

"This award represents the fruit of patient industry and perseverance. Some lucky people are natural born painters, but my talent only got me through the beginning stages of learning my craft. But no matter how many times my paintings failed to live up to my own standards, I never gave up. And no matter how much my painting improved—I was never satisfied. I'm still not, even though the Society of Illustrators was generous enough to recognize my work. It's wonderful to win this award—all the more so as it comes from people of such experience and discernment. Maybe someday I'll win a gold medal."

252

Artist: **Kadir Nelson**

Art Director: Howard Smiley

Client: Polygram Special Markets

Medium: Oil on canvas

Size: 28" x 36"

"When I played Little League baseball, once there was a substitute ump brought in to call the game. He was built like Santa Claus and had a southern accent. Every time the batter swung and missed or the pitcher threw a strike, the ump would yell out 'Streeeerack!!' We all laughed each time. So I named this painting after his exclamation. The painting portrays the Memphis Red Sox versus the Baltimore Elite Giants of the old Negro Leagues."

253

Artist: **Gary Kelley**

Art Director: Gary Kelley

Client: Orquesta Alto Maiz

Medium: Pastel on paper

Size: 16" x 16"

254

Artist: **Cathleen Toelke**

Art Director: Jim Branham

Client: Dana Communications

Medium: Gouache on watercolor board

Size: 6" x 7"

255

Artist: **Brad Holland**

Art Director: Roxy Moffit

Client: Seattle Repertory Theatre

Medium: Acrylic on masonite

Size: 19" x 24"

256

Artist: **Paul Zwolak**

Art Directors: Peter Schaefer, Andrea Costa

Client: The New York Times

Size: 15" x 20"

257

Artist: **Paul Zwolak**

Art Director: Tom Beebe

Client: Paul Stuart Store

Size: 18" x 14"

253

254

255

256

257

258

Artist: **Sally Wern Comport**

Art Director: Lesley Foster

Agency: Robin Shepherd Studios

Client: Accustaff Incorporated

Medium: Pastel, watercolor, charcoal
on coquille

Size: 12" x 16"

259

Artist: **Sally Wern Comport**

Art Director: Mark Litos

Agency: Litos Advertising & Design

Client: Parke Industries, Inc.

Medium: Pastel, watercolor, charcoal
on pastel cloth

Size: 12" x 18"

260

Artist: **Robert Neubecker**

Client: Kabelrheydt AG

Medium: Watercolor on paper

261

Artist: **Jordin Isip**

Art Director: Chad Dziewior

Client: Threadbare

Medium: Mixed on paper

Size: 21" x21"

262

Artist: **Wilson McLean**

Art Director: Lyle Metzdorf

Agency: Metzdorf Inc.

Medium: Oil on canvas

Size: 30" x 24"

263

Artist: **John H. Howard**

Art Directors: Sheryl Yasgar, Nancy Owens

Client: Dean Witter Reynolds

Medium: Acrylic on canvas

Size: 54" x 36"

258

259

260

261

262

263

264

Artist: **Stasys Eidrigevicius**

Art Director: Lance Barton

Client: World Beat Festival

Medium: Pastel on paper

265

Artist: **Wiktor Sadowski**

Art Director: James Seacat

Client: Actors Theatre of Louisville

Medium: Acrylic on canvas

266

Artist: **Andre Brown**

Art Director: Andre Brown

Client: Sanofi Pharmaceuticals

Medium: Colored pencil, pastel on masonite

Size: 16" x 6"

267

Artist: **Mark Ulriksen**

Art Director: Beth Harding

Agency: Wieden & Kennedy

Client: Nike

Medium: Acrylic on canvas

Size: 9 1/2" x 10"

268

Artist: **Hiro Kimura**

Art Director: Jill Bossert

Client: Society of Illustrators

Medium: Acrylic on board

Size: 11" x 13"

264

265

266

267

268

274

Artist: **Martin Jarrie**

Art Director: Lynn Brofsky

Client: Nordstrom

Size: 12" x 10"

275

Artist: **Steven Guarnaccia**

Art Director: Italo Lupi

Client: Campeggi

Medium: Pen & ink, watercolor on watercolor paper

276

Artist: **David Shannon**

Art Director: Ria Lewerke

Client: Ria Images

Medium: Acrylic, prismacolor on board

Size: 24" x 18"

277

Artist: **Chris Spollen**

Medium: Digital

Size: 14" x 11"

278

Artist: **Joel Nakamura**

Art Director: Cindi Troupin

Client: Jazziz

Medium: Acrylic on tooled tin

Size: 12" x 12"

279

Artist: **Ward Sutton**

Client: Artrock

Medium: Silkscreen on paper

Size: 35" x 22"

280

Artist: **Marcos Sorensen**

Art Director: Jason Skinner

Agency: Toth Advertising

Client: Union Bay Jeans

Medium: Digital

Size: 9" x 7"

274

275

276

277

278

279

280

286

Artist: **David O'Keefe**

Art Directors: Glenn Peltz, Cameron Dilley

Client: Waffle House (Northlake Foods)

Medium: Clay, digital

Size: 9" x 15"

287

Artist: **Bill Mayer**

Art Director: Carolyn Hoth

Client: Glennon

Medium: Gouache, dyes on board

Size: 11" x 12"

288

Artist: **Bill Mayer**

Art Director: Matthew Norman

Medium: Gouache, dyes on board

Size: 12" x 9"

289

Artist: **Larry McEntire**

Art Directors: Stan McElrath,
Christopher Colton

Agency: Anderson Advertising

Client: San Antonio Golf Association

Medium: Acrylic on canvas

Size: 5" x 15"

290

Artist: **Bill Mayer**

Art Director: Kitty McGee

Client: Skyward Marketing

Medium: Gouache on board

Size: 8" x 9"

286

287

288

289

290

291

Artist: **Ted Wright**

Art Director: J. Hudson

Client: Boy Scouts of America

Medium: Silkscreen inks on paper

292

Artist: **Dennis Ziemienski**

Client: Sonoma Valley Film Festival

Medium: Acrylic on canvas

293

Artist: **Dennis Ziemienski**

Client: Manka's Inverness

Medium: Acrylic on canvas

294

Artist: **Dennis Ziemienski**

Art Director: Pat Summers

Agency: Summers-McCann

Client: Sonoma Valley Film Festival

Medium: Acrylic on canvas

291

292

293

294

295

Artist: **Nanette Biers**

Art Director: Susan Pate

Agency: Pate International

Client: Opus One Winery

Medium: Oil on canvas

Size: 24" x 17"

296

Artist: **Sarah Wilkins**

Size: 9" x 12"

297

Artist: **Calef Brown**

Art Director: Greg Ross

Client: A & M Records

Medium: Acrylic on board

Size: 18" x 13"

298

Artist: **Joe Ciardiello**

Art Directors: Tommy Steele, John O'Brien

Client: Capitol Records

Medium: Pen, watercolor on paper

Size: 15" x 16"

299

Artist: **Joe Ciardiello**

Art Directors: Tommy Steele, John O'Brien

Client: Capitol Records

Medium: Pen, watercolor on paper

Size: 15" x 14"

295

296

297

The Cocktail Combos.

298

Chicago Blues Masters vol.3

299

300

Artist: **Gary Wayne Golden**

Art Director: Kandy Jones

Client: Arkansas River Blues Festival

Medium: Digital: Adobe Photoshop
       on Mac-Iris (giclee) print

Size: 18" x 17"

301

Artist: **Francis Livingston**

Art Director: Jennifer Coles

Client: The Atlantic Monthly

Medium: Oil on board

302

Artist: **John H. Howard**

Art Director: Mark Larson

Client: Warner Bros. Records

Medium: Acrylic on canvas

Size: 24" x 24"

303

Artist: **Kari Kroll**

Art Director: Kim Baer

Client: UCLA Theatre

Medium: Mixed, collage

Size: 16" x 11"

304

Artist: **Will Wilson**

Art Director: Nancy Donald

Client: Sony Music

Medium: Oil on canvas

300

301

302

303

304

305

Artist: **Charles Santore**

Art Director: Mark Giambrone

Client: Baldwin Piano Company

Medium: Watercolor on Arches

Size: 15" x 20"

306

Artist: **Diane Teske Harris**

Art Director: Rudy Resta

Client: The New York Times

Medium: Watercolor on board

Size: 19" x 9"

307

Artist: **Luba Lukova**

Client: Affinity Productions

Medium: Silkscreen on paper

Size: 41" x 29"

308

Artist: **Luba Lukova**

Client: Vineyard Theatre

Medium: Silkscreen

Size: 41" x 29"

309

Artist: **Luba Lukova**

Client: The Living Theatre

Medium: Silkscreen on craft paper

Size: 41" x 29"

305

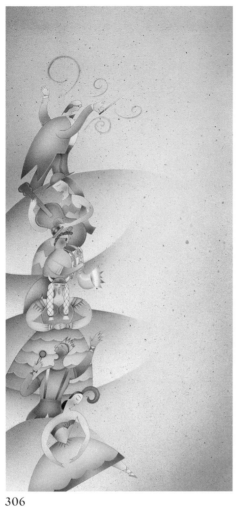

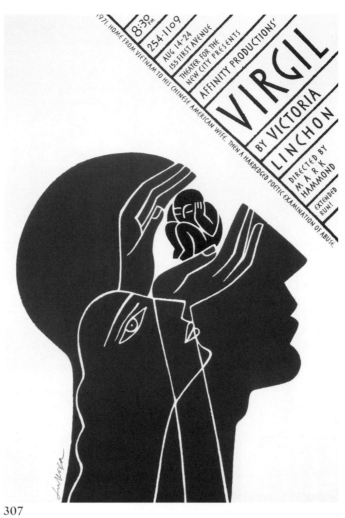

306

307

308

309

310

Artist: **David Lance Goines**

Client: Berkeley Horticultural Nursery

Medium: Solid color photo-offset lithography

Size: 24" x 17"

311

Artist: **Scott McKowen**

Client: Arena Stage

Medium: Scratchboard

Size: 8" x 7"

312

Artist: **Mark Summers**

Art Director: George Vogt

Agency: Sandstrom Design

Client: Yale New Haven Health

Medium: Scratchboard

Size: 8" x 8"

313

Artist: **Mark Summers**

Art Director: George Vogt

Agency: Sandstrom Design

Client: Yale New Haven Health

Medium: Scratchboard

Size: 9" x 7"

314

Artist: **Jack Unruh**

Art Director: Bill Carson

Client: Alex Sheshunoff Management
Services Inc.

Medium: Ink, watercolor on board

315

Artist: **Joe Ciardiello**

Art Director: Tommy Steele, John O'Brien

Client: Capitol Records

Medium: Pen, watercolor on paper

Size: 14" x 14"

310

311

312

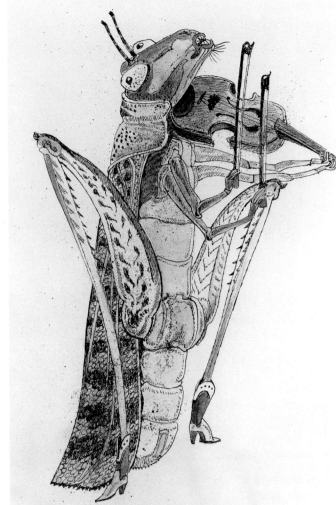

314

313

315

316

Artist: **Greg Dearth**

Art Director: Mike Ticcino

Client: P.D.C.

Medium: Scratchboard

Size: 9" x 13"

317

Artist: **Murray Tinkelman**

Art Director: Joe Glisson

Client: Dellas Graphics

Medium: Pen & ink on Bristol

Size: 13" x 10"

318

Artist: **Russell Farrell**

Art Director: Jay Cooper

Agency: Archer-Malmo

Client: Panther Woods

Medium: Acrylic on board

319

Artist: **Neil Shapiro**

Art Director: Kelly Ludden

Agency: Fasone Garrett Boehm

Client: Kansas City Area
　　　Transportation Authority

Medium: Graphite, oil, colored
　　　pencil on paper

Size: 17" x 9"

320

Artist: **John Ferry**

Art Directors: Kevin Swanson, John Ferry

Client: Kansas City Art Institute

Medium: Oil on masonite

Size: 11" x 9"

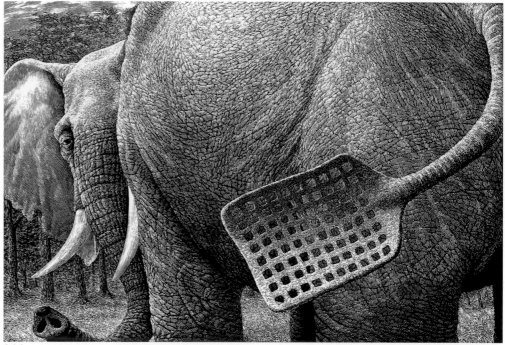

316

317

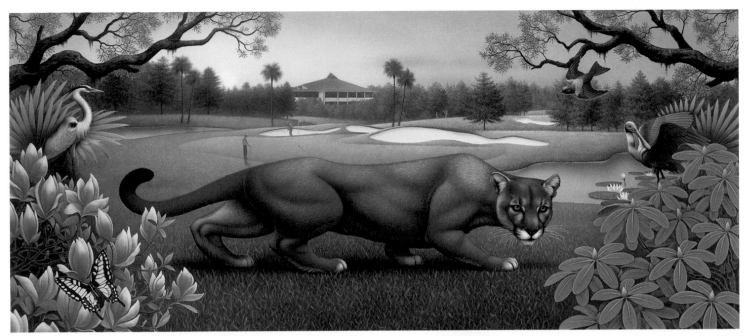

318

319

320

321

Artist: **Rick Farrell**

Art Director: Rick Farrell

Client: Rita Marie & Friends

Medium: Oil on board

Size: 37" x 25"

322

Artists: **Cheryl Greisbach, Stanley Martucci**

Art Directors: Richard Wilde, Rosie Rodrigues

Agency: Ryan Drossman & Partners

Client: Ryan Drossman & Partners

Medium: Oil

Size: 11" x 13"

323

Artist: **William Low**

Art Director: John Morton, Jean Wolf

Agency: Ammirati & Puris/Lintas

Client: Compaq Computers

Medium: Digital on rag paper

Size: 12" x 20"

324

Artist: **Bernie Fuchs**

Art Director: Karen Frost

Agency: Noble Associates

Client: Tyson

Medium: Oil on canvas

321

322

323

324

325
Artist: **Eugene Hoffman**
Medium: Cardboard

326
Artist: **Tom Nick Cocotos**
Art Director: Eric Neuner
Client: Columbia House
Medium: Collage on museum board
Size: 14" x 10"

327
Artist: **Tim O'Brien**
Art Director: Allison Schwartz
Client: CBS
Medium: Oil on panel
Size: 12" x 8"

328
Artist: **Rob Day**
Medium: Oil on paper
Size: 6" x 9"

329
Artist: **Dale Crawford**
Art Director: Craig Hamilton
Client: Opera Company of Philadelphia
Medium: Oil on paper
Size: 9" x 6"

330
Artist: **Marco Ventura**
Client: Sally Heflin & The Artworks
Medium: Oil on wood
Size: 5" x 7"

325

326

327

328

329

330

331

Artist: **Marco Ventura**

AClient: Maimeri

Medium: Oil on paper

Size: 13" x 20"

332

Artist: **Teresa Fasolino**

Art Director: Dan Marshall

Client: Poppe-Tyson

Medium: Oil on canvas

Size: 15" x 11"

333

Artist: **Anita Kunz**

Art Director: Frank Barrows

Client: Mutual Marine

Medium: Watercolor, gouache on board

334

Artist: **Robert Crawford**

Client: Original Zin

Medium: Acrylic on masonite

Size: 17" x 21"

335

Artist: **Greg Spalenka**

Client: Butthusker Music

Medium: Mixed on board

Size: 9" x 8"

331

332

333

334

335

336

Artist: **Marc Burckhardt**

Art Director: Janice Thompson

Client: MQbc

Medium: Acrylic on wood

Size: 17" x 16"

337

Artist: **Tom Bennett**

Art Director: Ada Whitney

Client: Showtime

Medium: Monotype on paper

*Size:*10" x 13"

338

Artist: **Theo Rudnak**

Art Director: Derek Rudnak

Medium: Gouache, acrylic on canvas

Size: 8" x 16"

339

Artist: **Peter de Sève**

Art Director: Peter LeDonne

Agency: LeDonne. Wilner & Weiner

Client: Livent

Medium: Watercolor, ink on watercolor paper

Size: 10" x 14"

340

Artist: **Peter de Sève**

Art Director: Peter LeDonne

Agency: LeDonne. Wilner & Weiner

Client: Livent

Medium: Watercolor, ink on watercolor paper

Size: 17" x 15"

336

337

339

338

340

341

Artist: **Paul Micich**

Art Director: Steve Sikova

Agency: Goodhue & Assoc.

Client: The Guthrie Theater

Medium: Alkyd on canvas

Size: 40" x 36"

342

Artist: **Kam Mak**

Art Directors: Al Cetta, Eric White

Client: HarperCollins

Medium: Oil on panel

Size: 13" x 20"

343

Artist: **Mark Ryden**

Art Directors: Jeff Fey, Tommy Steele

Client: Capitol Records

Medium: Oil on board

344

Artist: **Mark Ryden**

Art Directors: Jeff Fey, Tommy Steele

Client: Capitol Records

Medium: Oil on board

345

Artist: **Kinuko Craft**

Art Director: Kathleen Ryan

Client: Dallas Opera Company

Medium: Mixed on board

Size: 13" x 20"

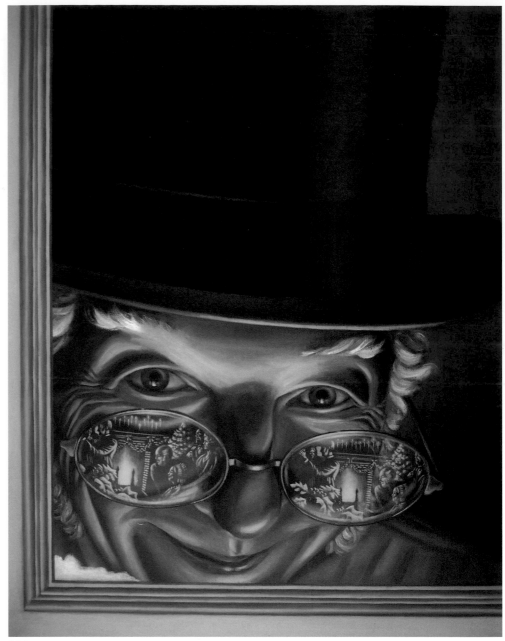

341

342

343

345

344

Teresa Fasolino
Chairman, Illustrator

Vaughn Andrews
Executive Art Director, Harcourt Brace

Peter de Sève
Illustrator

Bradford Hamann
Illustrator

Robert Hunt
Illustrator

Roger Kastel
Illustrator

Patrick Milbourn
Illustrator, Portrait painter

Jim Plumeri
Art Director, Bantam Books

Jeff Seaver
Illustrator

INSTITUTIONAL

AWARD
WINNERS

N. ASCENCIOS
Gold Medal

GARY KELLEY
Gold Medal

WILSON McLEAN
Gold Medal

JOHN ENGLISH
Silver Medal

JOEL PETER JOHNSON
Silver Medal

FRANCIS LIVINGSTON
Silver Medal

346

Artist: **N. Ascencios**

Medium: Oil on canvas

Size: 28" x 23"

"This message is brought to you by the letter N and the number 3."

347

Artist: **Gary Kelley**

Art Director: Gary Kelley

Client: Waverly Publishing

Medium: Pastel on paper

Size: 16" x 21"

This is Gary Kelley's fifth image for the Waverly Printing Company's annual calendar. He found inspiration in Robert Henri's *The Art Spirit*: "Beauty is the sensation of pleasure on the mind of the seer." He altered an old fashion shot and had some fun with the palette, then added an underlying line to jog the seer.

348

Artist: **Wilson McLean**

Art Director: Dave Dearman

Client: Boots and the Newborn Group

Medium: Oil on canvas

Size: 28" x 19"

"This landscape of fruit and flowers was a lengthy experience to complete; it has at least 30% more floral abundance than I wished to paint. The client insisted on more, more, more and brighter, brighter, brighter, which I of course complied with—they were holding my daughter hostage! So, if I had painted this picture in a more parsimonious way, as I wished, perhaps there would be no medal."

349

Artist: **John English**

Art Director: Kevin Pistilli

Client: The Raphael Hotel

Medium: Oil on canvas

Size: 24" x 17"

"I am honored to receive this award, especially for this particular piece. This painting was the first in a series of twelve regional landscapes. The client chose me as the artist for the project after seeing a group of my personal paintings and then gave me total creative control. The experience was wonderful and the award makes it just that much better."

350

Artist: **Joel Peter Johnson**

Art Director: Jessica Helfand

Client: AIGA

Medium: Oil on board

Size : 9" x 8"

Joel Peter Johnson is a freelance illustrator from New York who now makes his home in Houston, Texas. He graduated from the University at Buffalo in 1987 with a BFA in Painting and Illustration. With his fine art approach to conceptual illustration, Johnson reinvents traditional clichés with conceptual images that resemble moody Renaissance frescoes. Johnson's work has been exhibited nationally, including the Albright-Knox Art Gallery and Buffalo's Burchfield Art Center. Included in the Society's Annual Exhibitions since 1988, his work is part of the M&T Bank Collection at the Burchfield Art Center.

351

Artist: **Francis Livingston**

Client: Thomas R. Reynolds Fine Art

Medium: Oil on board

Size: 24" x 18"

"I've been painting the Santa Cruz Beach boardwalk for years. It instantly takes me back to a simple fun time. The Giant Dipper comes from the days when roller coasters were made of wood and creaked and swayed when you rode them. What I've tried to capture here is the moment that both thrilled and terrified people."

352

Artist: **David Brier**

Art Director: David Brier

Client: DBD International, Ltd

Medium: Digital: Adobe Illustrator on MAC

Size: 19" x 26"

353

Artist: **Vern Dufford**

Art Director: Ken Patrick

Medium: Oil, pastel on board

Size: 15" x 13"

354

Artist: **Vern Dufford**

Art Director: Ken Patrick

Medium: Oil, pastel on board

Size: 15" x 13"

355

Artist: **Cary Austin**

Art Director: David Usher

Client: The Greenwich Workshop

Medium: Acrylic on clayboard

352

353

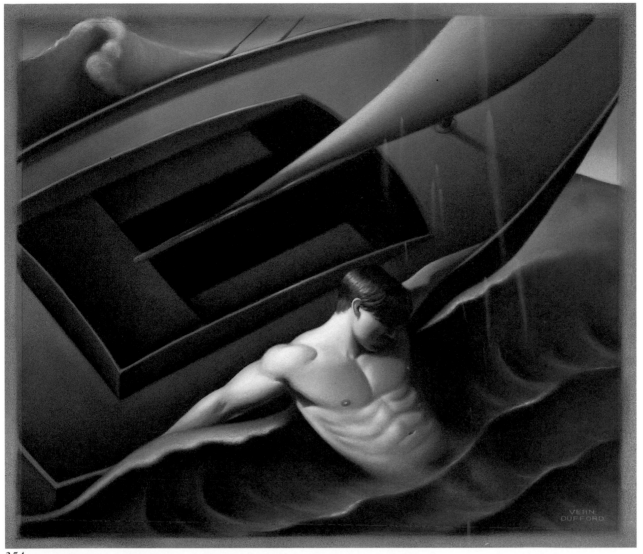

354

355

356

Artist: **Gary Kelley**

Art Director: Gary Kelley

Client: College Hill Arts Festival

Medium: Pastel on paper

Size: 24" x 20"

357

Artist: **Loren Long**

Art Director: Tracy Long

Client: Hamilton Stands

Medium: Acrylic on board

Size: 12" x 16"

358

Artist: **Martin French**

Art Director: Tom Thornton

Agency: The Mednick Group

Client: Rockport

Medium: Ink, acrylic, digital

Size: 16" x 22"

359

Artist: **Martin French**

Art Director: Martin French

Client: Northwest Reach

Medium: Ink, acrylic, digital: Adobe
            Photoshop (Iris Print)

Size: 12" x 20"

360

Artist: **Mark Covell**

Medium: Ink, Oil on board

Size:: 18" x 15"

356

357

358

359

360

361

Artist: **James McMullan**

Client: Leukemia Society of America

Medium: Gouache on paper

Size: 12" x 10"

362

Artist: **Jack Unruh**

Art Director: Horacio Cobos

Client: Baker Press

Medium: Ink, watercolor on board

Size: 17" x 13"

363

Artist: **Bill James**

Medium: Pastel on watercolor board

364

Artist: **Robert McGinnis**

Medium: Oil on masonite

Size: 15" x 21"

365

Artist: **Marvin Mattelson**

Art Director: Ann McFarlin

Client: Proformix

Medium: Oil on ragboard

Size: 6" x 7"

361

362

363

364

365

371

Artist: **James Bennett**

Medium: Oil over acrylic on board

Size: 10" x 8"

372

Artist: **James Bennett**

Medium: Oil over acrylic on board

Size: 9" x 7"

373

Artist: **James Bennett**

Art Director: Richard Solomon

Medium: Oil over acrylic on board

Size: 15" x 10"

374

Artist: **Murray Tinkelman**

Art Director: Murray Tinkelman

Client: Barnum Museum

Medium: Pen & ink on Bristol

Size: 11" x 14"

371

372

373

374

380

Artist: **Jack E. Davis**

Medium: Colored pencil on BFK
watercolor paper

Size: 12" x 9"

381

Artist: **Jack E. Davis**

Medium: Colored pencil on BFK
watercolor paper

Size: 13" x 10"

382

Artist: **Roberto Parada**

Medium: Oil on board

Size: 15" x 9"

383

Artist: **Roberto Parada**

Medium: Oil on board

Size: 15" x 11"

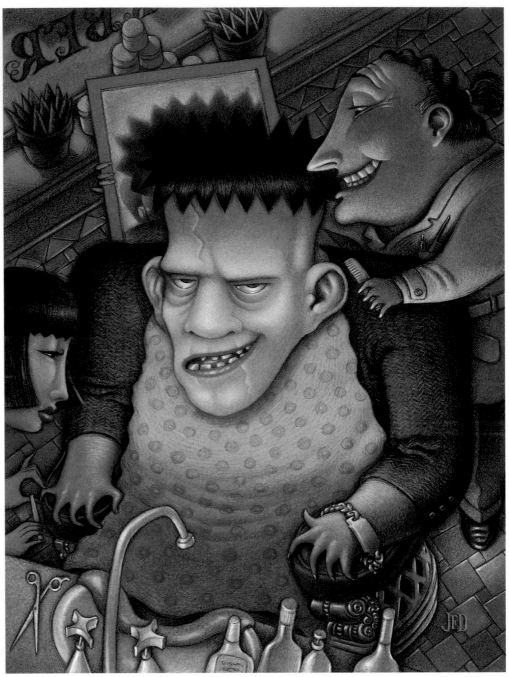

380

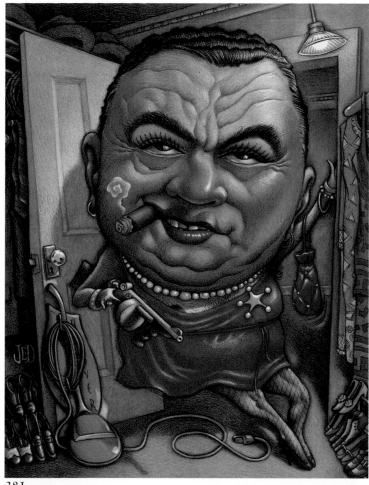

381

382

383

384

Artist: **Allan M. Burch**

Medium: Acrylic on board

Size: 18" x 15"

385

Artist: **Max Ginsburg**

Medium: Oil on masonite

Size: 10" x 7"

386

Artist: **Johanna St. Clair**

Medium: Gouache on paper

Size: 7" x 5"

387

Artist: **Mark Summers**

Art Director: Richard Solomon

Client: Richard Solomon Artists Rep.

Medium: Scratchboard, watercolor
          on board with overlay

Size: 10" x 7"

384

385

386

387

388

Artist: **Joe Ciardiello**

Client: The Alternative Pick

Medium: Pen & ink on paper

Size: 14" x 8"

389

Artist: **Michael J. Deas**

Art Director: Carl Herrman

Client: U.S. Postal Service

Medium: Oil on paper

Size: 8" x 5"

390

Artist: **Burt Silverman**

Art Director: Howard Paine

Client: U.S. Postal Service

Medium: Oil on panel

Size: 5" x 6"

391

Artist: **Burt Silverman**

Art Director: Howard Paine

Client: U.S. Postal Service

Medium: Oil on pane

Size: 5" x 6"

388

389

390

391

392

Artist: **Thomas Blackshear**

Art Director: Derry Noyes

Client: U.S. Postal Service

Medium: Watercolor, gouache on board

Size: 6" x 5"

393

Artist: **Thomas Blackshear**

Art Director: Derry Noyes

Client: U.S. Postal Service

Medium: Watercolor, gouache on board

Size: 6" x 5"

394

Artist: **William Phillips**

Art Director: Phil Jordan

Client: U.S. Postal Service

Medium: Oil on panel

Size: 10" x 12"

395

Artist: **James Gurney**

Art Director: Carl Herrman

Client: U.S. Postal Service

Medium: Oil on Bristol board

Size: 8" x 23"

392

393

394

395

396

Artist: **Greg Harlin**

Client: Whitmore Printing

Medium: Gouache, acrylic on board

Size: 12" x 21"

397

Artist: **Larry Moore**

Art Director: Jeff Morris

Client: Disney Design

Medium: Pastel on paper

398

Artist: **Brad Holland**

Art Director: Karen Landrigan

Agency: Smith & Associates

Client: Canadian Occidental Petroleum Ltd.

Medium: Acrylic on masonite

Siz:e 18" x 12"

399

Artist: Yvonne Buchanan

Medium: Watercolor, ink on paper

Size: 9" x 9"

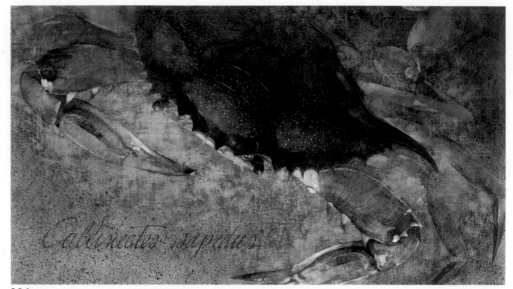

396

397

398

399

405

Artist: **Gregory Manchess**

Art Director: Stephen Koch

Agency: Manger & Associates, Inc.

Client: St. Agnes Healthcare

Medium: Oil on linen

Size: 20" x 15"

406

Artist: **Ted Wright**

Art Director: Pete Anderson

Client: Little Dog Records

Medium: Silkscreen inks on paper

Size: 12" x 12"

407

Artist: **Greg Dearth**

Client: Scott Hull Associates

Medium: Scratchboard

Size: 11" x 11"

405

406

407

408

Artist: **Braldt Bralds**

Art Director: David Usher, Braldt Bralds

Client: The Greenwich Workshop

Medium: Oil on masonite

Size: 8" x 8"

409

Artist: **Braldt Bralds**

Art Director: David Usher, Braldt Bralds

Client: The Greenwich Workshop

Medium: Oil on masonite

Size: 8" x 8"

410

Artist: **Richard Cowdrey**

Art Director: Tom Hough

Agency: Sibley Peteet Design

Client: Sibley Peteet Design

Medium: Acrylic on board

Size: 8" x 13"

411

Artist: **Mark Braught**

Medium: Pastel on paper

Size: 24" x 18"

412

Artist: **Braldt Bralds**

Art Director: David Usher, Braldt Bralds

Client: The Greenwich Workshop

Medium: Oil on masonite

Size: 25" x 35"

408

409

410

411

412

413

Artist: **Kari Alberg**

Art Director: Heather Cooley

Agency: Parachute, Inc.

Client: Children's Health Care Foundation

Medium: Watercolor on linoleum

Size: 11" x 14"

414

Artist: **Adam Gustavson**

Art Director: C.F. Payne

Medium: Mixed on paper

Size: 17" x 17"

415

Artist: **Hiro Kimura**

Medium: Oil

Size: 11" x 14"

416

Artist: **Jerry LoFaro**

Art Director: Jeff Varasano

Client: Funraisers USA

Medium: Acrylic on board

Size: 17" x 13"

417

Artist: **James Gurney**

Art Director: Collette Carter

Client: Portal Publications

Medium: Oil on canvas mounted on board

Size: 19" x 57"

413

414

415

416

417

418

Artist: **Mark Mille**

Medium: Oil on canvas

Size: 29" x 18"

419

Artist: **David Bowers**

Medium: Oil on masonite

Size: 13" x 17"

420

Artist: **John Rush**

Art Directors: Don Branch, Lou Sideris

Client: U.S. National Park Service

Medium: Oil on canvas

421

Artist: **Gary Godbee**

Medium: Oil on canvas

Size: 18" x 14"

422

Artist: **Michael J. Deas**

Art Director: Warren Luch

Client: Church of Latter-Day Saints

Medium: Oil on panel

418

419

420

421

422

423

Artist: **Kathy Lawrence**

Art Director: Dan Forst

Client: American Greetings

Medium: Oil on vidalon

Size: 16" x 10"

424

Artist: **Thomas Reis**

Medium: Oil on board

Size: 25" x 19"

425

Artist: **Daniel Adel**

Art Director: David Harris

Client: Vanity Fair

Medium: Oil on panel

Size: 14" x 17"

426

Artist: **Ernest Norcia**

Art Director: Martha Roelandt

Client: Creative Services

Medium: Charcoal, acrylics, tempera,
          oil glazes on gessoed board

Size: 17" x 23"

423

424

425

426

427

Artist: **Rafal Olbinski**

Art Director: Rita Marshall

Client: Creative Editions

Medium: Acrylic on linen

Size: 32" x 22"

428

Artist: **Norman Green**

Client: Laurel Collection

Medium: Watercolor on Arches
300 lb. cold press

Size: 20" x 28"

429

Artist: **Jerry LoFaro**

Medium: Acrylic, airbrush on board

Size: 9" x 12"

430

Artist: **Greg Spalenka**

Art Director: Anthony Padilla

Client: Art Institute of Southern California

Medium: Digital

Size: 15" x 12"

427

428

430

429

431

Artist: **Patrick Arrasmith**

Medium: Mixed on Bristol

Size: 30" x 17"

432

Artist: **John Rush**

Client: Eleanor Ettinger Gallery

Medium: Oil on canvas

433

Artist: **Bart Forbes**

Art Director: Milton Aschner

Client: Ussery Printing Co.

Medium: Oil on canvas

Size: 15" x 13"

434

Artist: **David Bowers**

Medium: Oil on masonite

431

432

433

434

440

Artist: **Frances Jetter**

Art Directors: Bridget Booher, Maxine Mills

Client: Duke Magazine

Medium: Linocut, metal on paper

Size: 12" x 15"

441

Artist: **Alan E. Cober**

Medium: Clay, glaze

442

Artist: **Mike Harris**

Art Director: Scott Bieser

Client: Interplay, Inc.

Medium: Digital

Size: 10" x 6"

443

Artist: **Marc Phares**

Client: Epic Studios, Inc.

Medium: Digital Iris Print (output)

Size: 8" x 10"

444

Artist: **Marc Phares**

Client: Epic Studios, Inc.

Medium: Digital Iris Print (output)

Size: 10" x 15"

440

441

442

443

444

449

Artist: **John Craig**

Art Director: Gorden Mortensen

Client: Informix

Medium: Collage, digital

Size: 10" x 14"

450

Artist: **John Craig**

Art Director: Gorden Mortensen

Client: Informix

Medium: Collage, digital

Size: 11" x 11"

451

Artist: **Larry Moore**

Art Director: Steve Carsella

Agency: Backbone Design

Client: Creative Club of Orlando

Medium: Pastel on paper

Size: 10" x 15"

452

Artist: **Robert Hunt**

Art Director: Debra Bandelin

Client: Syracuse University

Medium: Oil on paper

Size: 27" x 18"

449

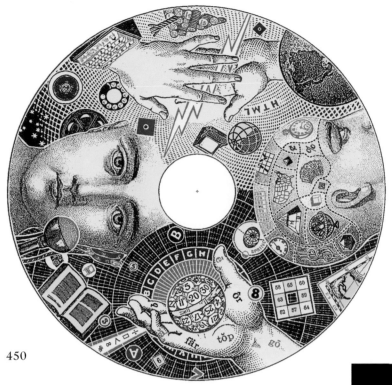

450

451

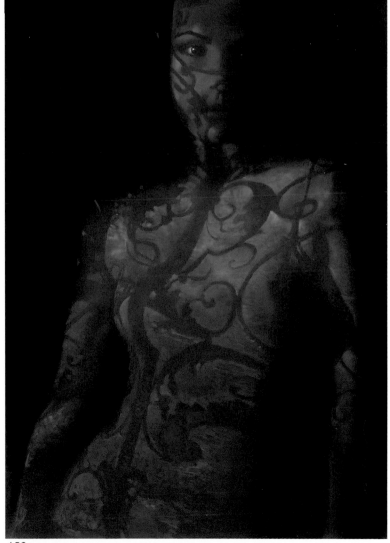

452

453

Artist: **Martin French**

Art Director: Alyce Heath

Client: Society of Illustrators - LA

Medium: Ink, acrylic, digital: Adobe
Photoshop (Iris Print)

Size: 8" x 7"

454

Artist: **Karen Santry**

Art Directors: John Burns III,
Grosa & Alex Leong

Client: N.V.A. Posters

Medium: Oil on canvas

Size: 45" x 30"

455

Artist: **Jerry Moriarty**

Art Director: Silas H. Rhodes

Client: School of Visual Arts

Medium: Oil on linen

Size: 48" x 32"

456

Artist: **David Wilcox**

Art Directors: Karen Lukas-Hardy, Paula Scher

Client: The Newborn Group

Medium: Acrylic on hardboard

Size: 19" x 19"

453

454

455

456

457

Artist: **Wilson McLean**

Medium: Oil on canvas

Size: 16" x 22"

458

Artist: **David Wilcox**

Art Directors: Karen Lukas-Hardy, Paula Scher

Client: The Newborn Group

Medium: Acrylic on masonite

Size: 22" x 17"

459

Artist: **Robert Giusti**

Art Directors: Joan Sigman, Mark Hess

Client: The Newborn Group

Medium: Acrylic on linen

Size: 12" x 19"

460

Artist: **Craig Frazier**

Art Director: Craig Frazier

Client: Target Direct Impressions

Medium: Cut Amberlith/Digital

Size: 11" x 33"

457

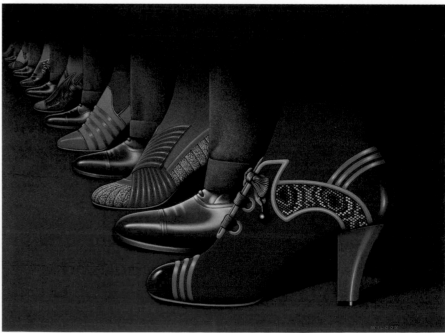

458

459

460

466

Artist: **Robert J. Barber**

Art Directors: Chris Krueger, Melissa Posen

Client: American Museum of Natural History

Medium: Archival flexible oils on canvas

467

Artist: **David Febland**

Medium: Oil, alkyd on acrylic ground
         on linen

Size: 30" x 36"

468

Artist: **Francis Livingston**

Client: Thomas R. Reynolds Fine Art

Medium: Oil on board

Size: 24" x 18"

469

Artist: **Bob Crofut**

Medium: Oil on canvas

Size: 34" x 22"

466

467

468

469

474

Artist: **William Westman**

Medium: Oil on panel

Size: 18" x 22"

475

Artist: **Michael R. Powell**

Client: Joe Esposito and Sons, Inc.

Medium: Acrylic on ragboard

Size: 8" x 9"

476

Artist: **Cyril David**

Medium: Graphite on paper

Size: 9" x 19"

477

Artist: **Gretchen Dow Simpson**

Medium: Acrylic

Size: 18" x 17"

474

475

476

477

483

Artist: **John P. Maggard III**

Client: Scott Hull Associates

Medium: Acrylic, oil on Strathmore

Size: 24" x 18"

484

Artist: **David Febland**

Medium: Oil, alkyd on acrylic ground
         on linen

Size: 28" x 22"

485

Artist: **John Ferry**

Art Director: John Ferry

Client: Massman Gallery, Rockhurst College

Medium: Oil on masonite

Size: 15" x 11"

483

484

485

486

Artist: **Allan M. Burch**

Medium: Acrylic on board

Size: 18" x 12"

487

Artist: **Sean Beavers**

Medium: Oil on linen

Size: 11" x 22"

488

Artist: **Kazuhiko Sano**

Medium: Acrylic, mixed on board

Size: 24" x 22"

486

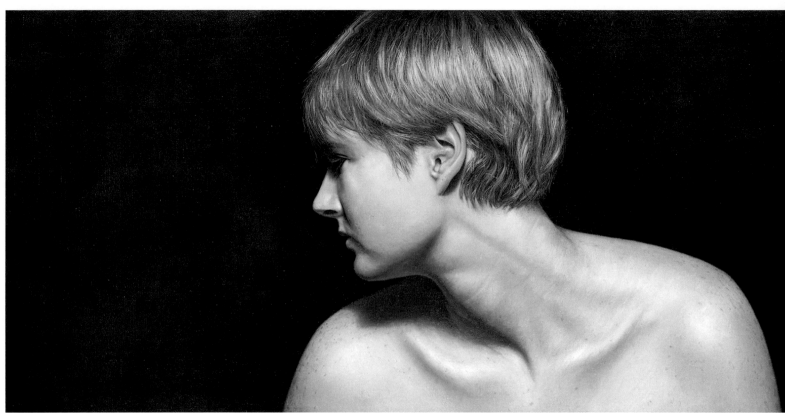

487

488

489

Artist: **Robert Hunt**

Size: 40" x 24"

490

Artist: **Kazuhiko Sano**

Medium: Acrylic on gessoed board

Size: 35" x 26"

491

Artist: **Kazuhiko Sano**

Medium: Acrylic, mixed

Size: 35" x 26"

492

Artist: **Bill James**

Medium: Pastel on Canson Mi-Tienties paper

Size: 32" x24"

493

Artist: **Patrick D. Milbourn**

Medium: Pastel on paper

Size: 13" x 9"

489

490

492

491

493

498

Artist: **Tim O'Brien**

Art Director: Joe Kimberling

Client: The International
Buster Keaton Society

Medium: Oil on board

Size: 18" x 14"

499

Artist: **Bernie Fuchs**

Art Director: Nicola Elstone

Client: Royal Caribbean

Medium: Oil on canvas

500

Artist: **David Meikle**

Art Director: Scott Greer

Client: University of Utah
Development Office

Medium: Acrylic on paper

Size: 10" x 12"

501

Artist: **Harry F. Bliss**

Medium: Watercolor on Arches
watercolor paper

Size: 6" x 9"

498

499

500

501

507

Artist: **Joe Sorren**

Medium: Acrylic on canvas

Size: 35" x 23"

508

Artist: **Mark A. Fredrickson**

Medium: Acrylic

Size: 16" x 13"

509

Artist: **Sam Ward**

Art Director: Bill Chadbourne

Client: American Forces Information Service

Medium: Gouache on Bristol

Size: 20" x 21"

510

Artist: **Shelly Hehenberger**

Client: Simon & Schuster

Medium: Chalk pastel, colored pencils
on tinted Canson charcoal paper

Size: 14" x 10"

511

Artist: **David E. Lesh**

Art Director: Doug May

Client: Forbes Group

Medium: Mixed on board

Size: 9" x 11"

507

508

510

509

511

512

Artist: **James Fryer**

Art Director: Jack Rooke

Client: Rainbird Design Associates

Medium: Acrylic

Size: 30cm x 40cm

513

Artist: **Wim Heesakkers**

Art Director: A. Schipper

Client: Thieme

Size: 50cm x 70cm

514

Artist: **Miki Ishii**

Art Director: Miki Ishii

Client: Sony Music Entertainment, Inc.

Medium: Oil, collage on board

Size: 35cm x 45cm

515

Artist: **Miki Ishii**

Art Director: Minori Ichikawa

Client: Aoyama Publishing Co., Ltd.

Medium: Oil, collage on board

Size: 36cm x 51cm

516

Artist: **Miki Ishii**

Art Director: Miki Ishii

Client: Public Career Design Center

Medium: Oil, collage on board

Size: 36cm x 26cm

517

Artist: **Harvey Chan**

Art Director: Harvey Chan

Client: Public Groundwood Books

Medium: Pastel

Size: 36cm x 26cm

512

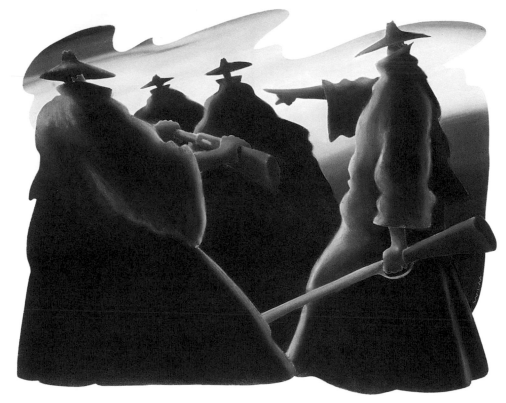

513

514

515

516

517

523

Artist: **Kazunori Kano**

Art Director: Kazunori Kano

Size: 40cm x 30cm

524

Artist: **Horacio Guerriero**

Art Director: Horacio Guerriero

Client: Galeria Latina

Size: 60cm x 80cm

525

Artist: **Susan Leopold**

Client: Homefront

Medium: Mixed

Size: 11" x 8"

526

Artist: **Horacio Guerriero**

Art Director: Horacio Guerriero

Client: Galeria Latina

Size: 60cm x 80cm

527

Artist: **Hitoshi Miura**

Art Director: Hitoshi Miura

Client: Miura Creations

Size: 16cm x 26cm

528

Artist: **Hitoshi Miura**

Art Director: Hitoshi Miura

Client: Japan Pulp and Paper Co., Ltd.

Size: 15cm x 28cm

529

Artist: **Michael Bramman**

Art Directors: Suzy and Nigel Atkins

Client: La Galerie Du Don

Medium: Acrylic

Size: 32cm x 50cm

523

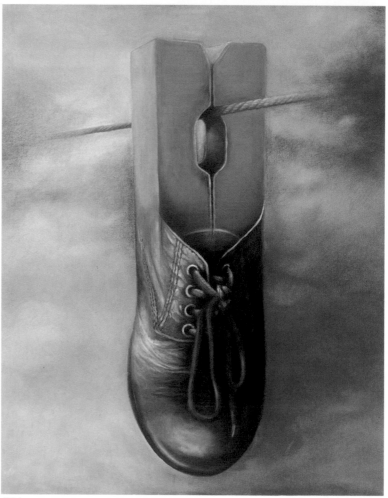

524

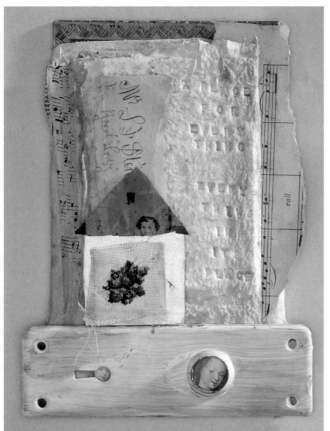

525

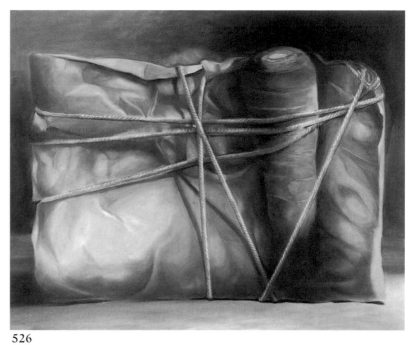

526

527

謹賀新年
1998年 元旦

ⓙ 日本紙パルプ商事株式会社

〒103-8641 東京都中央区日本橋本石町4-6-11　TEL.03-3270-1311（代表）

528

529

536

Artist: **Wayne Anderson**

Art Director: Robert Brown

Client: Screwloose Designs

Medium: Acrylic, coloured pencil, pencil

Size: 300cm x 240cm

537

Artist: **Jurgen Mick**

Medium: Colored pencil

Size: 32cm x 35cm

538

Artist: **Jurgen Mick**

Medium: Ink, colored pencil

Size: 43cm x 60cm

539

Artist: **Jamie Morris**

Medium: Pastel, gesso

Size: 27cm x 20cm

540

Artist: **Peter A. Wilkinson**

Art Director: Barry Oakly

Client: The Weekend Australian

Size: 25cm x 19cm

541

Artist: **Raul Arids**

Art Director: Carmelo Caderot

Medium: Ink

Size: 20cm x 35cm

536

537

538

540

539

541

549
Artist: **Kiyoko Yamazuki**
Art Director: Kiyoka Yamazuki
Size: 11cm X 15cm

550
Artist: **Kiyoko Yamazuki**
Art Director: Kiyoka Yamazuki
Size: 11cm X 15cm

551
Artist: **Louisa St. Pierre**
Art Director: Gill England
Client: Mother's Union
Medium: Mixed
Size: 25cm x 33cm

552
Artist: **Barbara Spurll**
Art Director: Barbara Spurll
Medium: Watercolor, dyes
Size: 41cm x 34cm

553
Artist: **Kestutis Kasparavicius**
Art Director: Hao, Kuang Tsai
Client: Grimm Press
Medium: Watercolor
Size: 29cm x 21cm

554
Artist: **Ricardo Martinez**
Art Director: Carmelo Caderot
Medium: Scratchboard, watercolor
Size: 11" x 9 3/4"

555
Artist: Peter Warner
Client: Hodder Children's Books
Medium: Watercolor
Size: 32cm x 23cm

556
Artist: **Kunio Sato**
Art Director: Tennoji Zoo
Size: 52cm x 73cm

557
Artist: **Peter A. Wilkinson**
Art Director: Barry Oakly
Size: 28cm x 29cm

558
Artist: **Carl Ellis**
Art Directors: Chris Yate, Jon Ward-Allen
Client: Waterlog Magazine
Medium: Watercolor
Size: 40cm x 40cm

549

550

551

552

553

554

555

556

558

557

Alan E. Cober (1935-1998) is credited with being a pioneer of expressionist illustration and a graphic journalist who initiated many important stories. The youngest to be named "Artist of the Year" by the Artists Guild in New York, Cober went on to win every major award in his field, including the prestigious Hamilton King Award from the Society of Illustrators. As a visual journalist he has covered such stories as the Pope's visit to the United States, the 1980 Presidential campaign and the shuttle lift off at Cape Canaveral. He presented a disturbing reality in his eloquent book "The Forgotten Society" which revealed life at the Willowbrook State Institution for the retarded, inmates at Sing Sing Prison, and the aged and dying in a nursing home. Much of his work dealt with themes of social significance forcing the viewer to come to terms with societal injustices.

Cober created a mural for the Smithsonian, raised corporate communication to an art form, completed editorial assignments for every major periodical and was an award winning children's book illustrator. His drawings and etchings have been exhibited in numerous one man and juried group shows and are in important national collections. Alan E. Cober was a passionate drawer, a consummate artist.

Cober practiced what he preached. Everywhere he traveled he created a body of work in a sketchbook. For every assignment he did the research necessary to inform his drawings, whether that information was found in a museum, library or on the street. He brought his passion for visual expression as a communicating art into the classroom.

Alan E. Cober was an exemplary artist/educator, who was willing to share with younger artists his wealth of experience, his passion for drawing, his love of life. He served as a role model in the true sense of practicing what he preached and he was highly successful at both.

Kathleen Collins Howell
University at Buffalo

Institutions at which Alan E. Cober taught:

The Illustrators Workshop
University at Buffalo, SUNY
University of Georgia
Ringling School of Art and Design

Alan is the second recipient of this
annual award selected by the
Board of Directors upon recommendation
of the Education Committee

HALLMARK CORPORATE FOUNDATION
MATCHING GRANTS

The Hallmark Corporate Foundation of Kansas City, Missouri, is again this year supplying full matching grants for all of the awards in the Society's Student Scholarship Competition. Grants, restricted to the Illustration Departments, are awarded to the following institutions:

13,500	Art Center College of Design
6,500	School of Visual Arts
4,000	Academy of Art College
3,000	Syracuse University
2,500	Columbus College of Art & Design
2,000	Paier College of Art
1,500	Pratt Institute
1,000	Lyme Academy of Fine Arts
1,000	Rhode Island School of Design

SCHOLARSHIP COMMITTEE AND JURY

COMMITTEE

Tim O'Brien, Chairman, N. Ascencios, MaryJane Begin, Teresa Fasolino, Lauren Uram

JURY

Melinda Beck *illustrator*, Tim Bower *illustrator*, Cheryl Checkman (Checkman Design Inc.), Pat Cummings *illustrator*, Margaret Cusack *illustrator*, Lisa Cyr *illustrator*, Gina Davis (A.D., *Good Housekeeping)* Andrea Dunham (A.D., *New York Magazine)*, Joanie Friedman (A.D., Berkley Books), Dave Goldin *illustrator*, Johanna Goodman *illustrator*, Mark Hess *illustrator*, Jordin Isip *illustrator*, Nicki Kalish (A.D., *New York Times, Sophisticated Traveler)*, Wilson McLean *illustrator*, Mike Mrak (A.D., *Content Magazine)*, Owen Phillips (A.D., *The New Yorker)*, Jennifer Presant (A.D., Scholastic, Inc.), Jessie Reyes (A.D., Penguin Books), Victoria Roberts *illustrator*, Burt Silverman *illustrator*, Philip Straub *illustrator*, Lauren Uram *illustrator*, Michael Witte *illustrator*

John J. Crockett
Vladimir Shpitalnik, Instructor
Paier College of Art
$2,000 The Greenwich Workshop Award

Enjeong Noh
David Mocarski, Instructor
Art Center College of Design
$2,500 The Starr Foundation Award
1999 "Call For Entries"
Poster Award

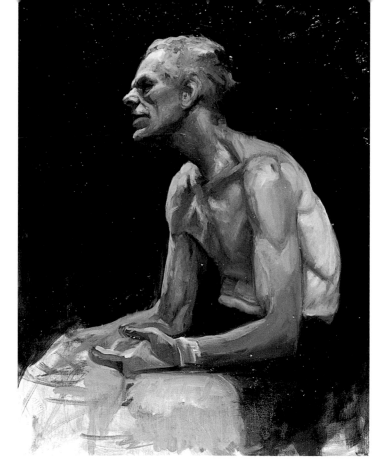

Nicolas Uribe-Benninghoff
Max Ginsburg, Instructor
School of Visual Arts
RSVP Publication Award

Seung Hong
William Moughan, Instructor
Academy of Art College
$2,000 Albert Dorne Award

Daisuke Tsutsumi
Max Ginsburg, Instructor
School of Visual Arts
$2,000 Albert Dorne Award

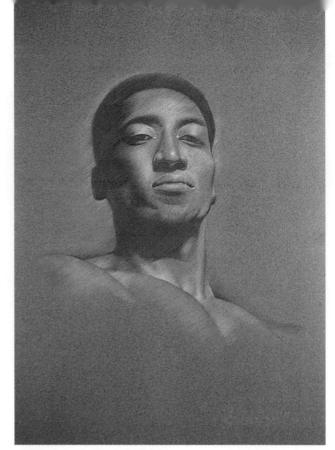

S. Christian DeLoach
John Thompson, Instructor
Syracuse University
$1,000 Dick Blick Art Materials Award

David Cho
James Wu, Instructor
Academy of Art College
$1,000 Award in Memory of Meg Wohlberg

Samuel Leshnick
Bob Kato, Instructor
Art Center College of Design
$1,000 Norma and Alvin Pimsler Award

Phung Huynh
Phil Hays, Instructor
Art Center College of Design
$1,000 The Norman Rockwell
Museum at Stockbridge Award

Eileen O'Connell
Linda Benson, Instructor
Syracuse University
$1,000 Award in Memory of
Augie Napoli

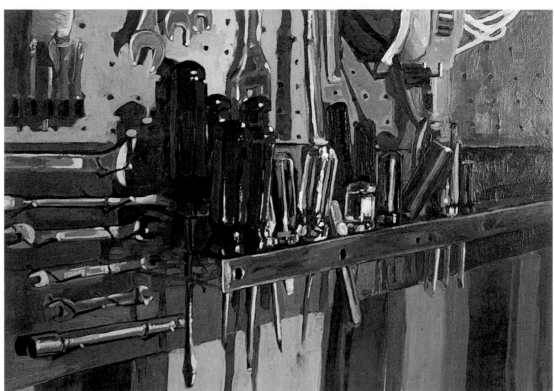

Dana S. Johnstone
Alex Bostic, Instructor
Virginia Commonwealth University

Gregory Krumm
Mark Thomas, Instructor
Art Academy of Cincinnati

Megan Johnson
Durwin Talon, Instructor
Savannah College of Art & Design

Eli McGinthia
John Ferry, Instructor
Kansas City Art Institute

Lawrence D. Nichols
Marilyn Rygg-Nordell
Art Institute of Seattle

Sotirios Rasiotis
Bob Dorsey, Instructor
Rochester Institute of Technology

Galen Montague
Bethanne Anderson, Instructor
Brigham Young University

Robert Sato
Halstead Hannah, Instructor
California College of Arts & Crafts

Jessica Lombardi
Suzanne Barnes, Instructor
Art Institute of Boston

Ron Powell
Karen Santry, Instructor
Jersey City State College

Nate Pack
Glen Edwards, Instructor
Utah State University

Haruno Shimodhira
Wendy Popp, Instructor
Parsons School of Design

V. Vachula
Herb Tauss, Instructor
Fashion Institute of Technology

Jose Portillo
Jerrold Bishop, Instructor
University of Arizona

Andre Treniek
Phil Singer, Instructor
University of the Arts

Joy Steuerwald
John Clapp, Instructor
San Jose State University

ARTIST INDEX

ARTIST INDEX

ARTIST INDEX

INTERNATIONAL ARTIST INDEX

Art Directors

INTERNATIONAL ART DIRECTORS, CLIENTS

PROFESSIONAL STATEMENTS

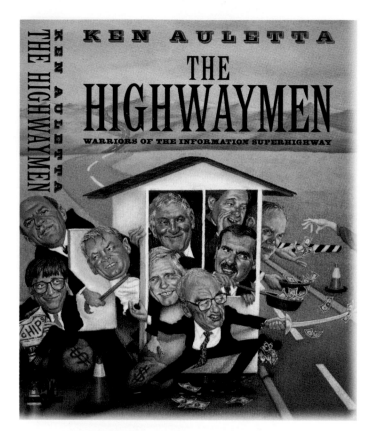

PATRICK D. MILBOURN

Artist
327 West 22 Street
New York, NY 10011
Tel/Fax (212) 989-4594

talent within

american

showcase

ZOË VILES

NEW YORK

•

SANTA FE

2 1 2 • 7 7 4 • 7 4 6 6

In a second
the hungry beast leapt
and attacked Swan fiercely.

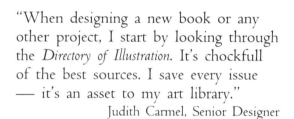

KIRCHOFF/WOHLBERG
ARTISTS REPRESENTATIVES

"An Evening at the Society of Illustrators"

866 United Nations Plaza New York, NY 10017

Phone: 212~644~2020 Fax: 212~223~4387 www.kirchoffwohlberg.com

KADIR NELSON

8 8 8 · 3 1 0 · 3 2 2 2

Mark BrAUgHT

404.373.7430 (fax)404.373.7433
767 North Parkwood Road
Decatur, Georgia 30030 USA

SOCIETY
ACTIVITIES

STEVAN DOHANOS AWARD Ted Lewin

OUR OWN SHOW
1998

THE SOCIETY OF ILLUSTRATORS
MEMBERS NINTH ANNUAL
OPEN EXHIBITION

"Our Own Show" is pleased to continue the Stevan Dohanos Award
as the Best in Show in this open, unjuried exhibition.

AWARD OF MERIT Robert McGinnis

"Our Own Show" was created to extend this annual opportunity for all professionally active members of the Society to exhibit a work in the Museum galleries. Each year nearly 200 artists participate.

"Our Own Show" is the major funding source for the Ten Year Rebuilding plan which is modernizing the Society's 1875 Carriage House headquarters for the 21st Century.

AWARD OF MERIT Donato Giancola

THE ORIGINAL ART 1998

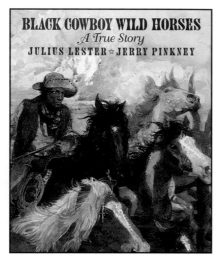

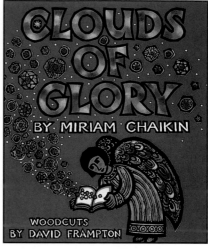

SILVER

Illustrator: *Jerry Pinkney*

Book: Black Cowboy, Wild Horses

Art Director: Atha Tehon

Editor: Phyllis Fogelman

Publisher: Dial Books for Young Readers

SILVER

Illustrator: *Denise Fleming*

Book: Time to Sleep

Art Director: Martha Rago

Editor: Laura Godwin

Publisher: Henry Holt and Co.

SILVER

Illustrator: *David Frampton*

Book: Clouds of Glory

Art Director: Anne Diebel

Editor: Dorothy Briley

Publisher: Houghton Mifflin/Clarion Books

Founded in 1980 to "Celebrate the Fine Art of Children's Book Illustration," this exhibition has been sponsored by the Society of Illustrators for the past eight years.

THE SELECTION PROCESS WAS BY A JURY OF OUTSTANDING ILLUSTRATORS, ART DIRECTORS AND EDITORS IN THE FIELD OF CHILDREN'S BOOK PUBLISHING.

JURY:

Anne Diebel • Ann Grifalconi • Christy Hale • Michael Patrick Hearn • Robert Sabuda • Edward Sorel

Betsy Lewin **CHAIR, "The Original Art 1998"**

Dilys Evans **FOUNDER, "The Original Art"**

JOIN THE SOCIETY OF ILLUSTRATORS
FOR THE PRICE OF A SPOT

© Gerry Gersten

For roughly the price of one tiny editorial illustration— and we all know
what that is—you can belong to the Society of Illustrators.

Illustrators, art directors, educators and those in related fields should be
part of this organization and are invited to apply. As space in this ad
is limited, we can't list all of the membership benefits, but contact
the Society and we'll send you the information.

SOCIETY OF ILLUSTRATORS

128 East 63rd Street • New York, NY 10021-7303 • (212) 838-2560 • fax (212) 838-2561
EMail: society@societyillustrators.org

SOCIETY OF ILLUSTRATORS MUSEUM SHOP

The Society of Illustrators Museum of American Illustration maintains a shop featuring many quality products. Four-color, large format books document contemporary illustration and the great artists of the past. Museum quality prints and posters capture classic images. T-shirts, sweatshirts, hats, mugs and tote bags make practical and fun gifts.

The Museum Shop is an extension of the Society's role as the center for illustration in America today. For further information or quantity discounts, contact the Society at
TEL: (212) 838-2560 / FAX: (212) 838-2561
EMail: society@societyillustrators.org

ILLUSTRATORS ANNUAL BOOKS

These catalogs are based on our annual juried exhibitions, divided into four major categories in American Illustration: Editorial, Book, Advertising, and Institutional. Some are available in a limited supply only.

In addition, a limited number of out-of-print collector's editions of the Illustrators Annuals that are not listed below (1959 to Illustrators 30) are available as is.

Also available for collectors are back issues of The Art Directors Club annuals and GRAPHIS Annuals.

Contact the Society for details...

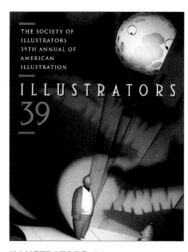

ILLUSTRATORS 39
$40.00

ILLUSTRATORS 38
$40.00

ILLUSTRATORS 40
320 pp.
Cover by Leo and Diane Dillon.
Contains 489 works of art.
Included are Hall of Fame biographies
and the Hamilton King interview.
Our most recent annual, the most contemporary illustration.
$57.50

NEW!

ILLUSTRATORS 37
$40.00

ILLUSTRATORS 36
$30.00

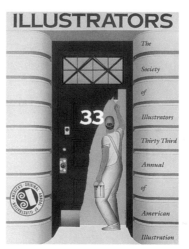

ILLUSTRATORS 33
$25.00
limited number remaining

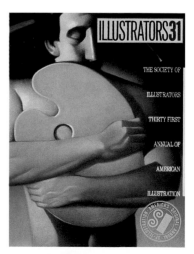

ILLUSTRATORS 31
$20.00
limited number remaining

SOCIETY OF ILLUSTRATORS • 128 East 63rd Street • New York, NY 10021-7303
www.societyillustrators.org

Raul Colòn

Jerry Pinkney

Guy Billout

Fred Otnes

ARTISTS FEATURED IN THE SERIES:

EDITORIAL

Marshall Arisman
Guy Billout
Alan E. Cober
Elaine Duillo
Joan Hall
Wilson McLean
Barbara Nessim
Tim O'Brien
Mel Odom

ADVERTISING

N. Ascencios
Mark Borow
Robert M. Cunningham
Teresa Fasolino
Mark Hess
Hiro Kimura
Rafal Olbinski
Fred Otnes
Chris Spollen

CHILDREN'S BOOKS

Steve Byram
Raul Colòn
Laura Cornell
Steve Kroninger
Emily McCully
James McMullan
Jerry Pinkney
Charles Santore
Dan Yaccarino

PRO-ILLUSTRATION
by Jill Bossert

A New How-to Series

$29.95 EACH. SET OF THREE $60.00

VOLUME ONE
EDITORIAL ILLUSTRATION

The Society of Illustrators has simulated an editorial assignment for a Sunday magazine supplement surveying the topic of "Love." Topics assigned to the illustrators include: Erotic Love, First Love, Weddings, Sensual Love, Computer Love, Adultery and Divorce. The stages of execution. from initial sketch to finish, are shown in a series of photographs and accompanying text. It's a unique, behind-the-scenes look at each illustrator's studio and the secrets of their individual styles. Professional techniques demonstrated include oil, acrylic, collage, computer, etching, trompe l'oeil, dyes and airbrush.

Joan Hall

Chris Spollen

VOLUME TWO
ADVERTISING ILLUSTRATION

This is an advertising campaign for a fictitious manufacturer of timepieces. The overall concept is "Time" and nine of the very best illustrators put their talents to solving the problem. The stages of execution, from initial phone call to finish, are described in photographs and text. You'll understand the demonstration of the techniques used to create a final piece of art. Professional techniques demonstrated include oil, acrylic, mixed media collage, computer, three-dimension and airbrush.

VOLUME THREE
CHILDREN'S BOOKS

In photographs and text, each of the nine artists describe the stages of execution from initial idea--if they are the author, too--or manuscript proposed by an editor, to the completion of a piece of art. They discuss the special challenges of creating children's books, among them: consistency of character and tone, attention to pace and visual flow, and the task of serving narrative as well as aesthetics.

Charles Santore

Maxfield Parrish • J. C. Leyendecker • Norman Rockwell • N. C. Wyeth • James Montgomery Flagg • Dean Cornwell
Harold Von Schmidt • Al Parker • Robert Fawcett • Stevan Dohanos • Tom Lovell • Charles Dana Gibson
Bernie Fuchs • Winslow Homer • Robert Peak • Coby Whitmore • Frederic Remington • Howard Chandler Christy
John Clymer • Mark English • Charles Marion Russell • Rockwell Kent • Al Hirschfeld • Haddon Sundblom
Maurice Sendak • René Bouché • Robert T. McCall • John Held, Jr. • Burt Silverman • Jessie Willcox Smith • Joe Bowler
Dorothy Hood • Robert McGinnis • Thomas Nast • Coles Phillips • Ben Shahn • McClelland Barclay
and many, many more

"The Glen," illustration for Brown & Bigelow calendar, 1938. Photo courtesy of the Archives of the American Illustrators Gallery, New York City.

Design for the Century Mid-Summer Holiday Number, August, 1897. Photo courtesy of the Archives of the American Illustrator Gallery, New York City.

"Garden of Allah," decoration for gift boxes of Crane's Chocolates, 1918. Photo courtesy of the Archives of the American Illustrators Gallery, New York City.

62

63

FAMOUS AMERICAN ILLUSTRATORS
THE HALL OF FAME

NEW!

by Arpi Ermoyan

Every year since the inception of the Hall of Fame in 1958, the Society of Illustrators bestows its highest honor upon those artists recognized for their distinguished achievement in the art of illustration. The 87 recipients of the Hall of Fame Award represented in this book are the foremost illustrators of the last two centuries.

FAMOUS AMERICAN ILLUSTRATORS, a full-color, 224 page volume, is a veritable "Who's Who" of American illustration. The artists are presented in the order in which they were elected to the Hall of Fame. Included are short biographical sketches and major examples of each artist's work. Their range of styles is all-encompassing, their viewpoints varied, their palettes imaginative. The changing patterns of life in America are vividly recorded as seen through the eyes of these men and women—the greatest illustrators of the 19th and 20th Centuries. **11 1-2 x 12 inches. $49.95**

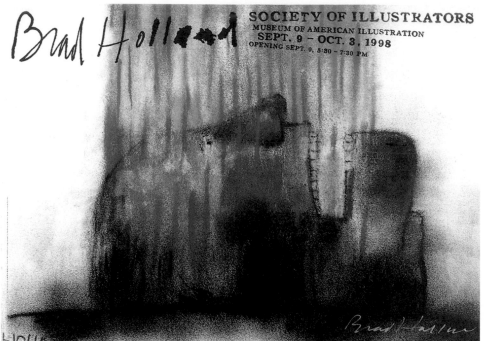

BRAD HOLLAND EXHIBITION 1998 - 34" x 24" $20.00

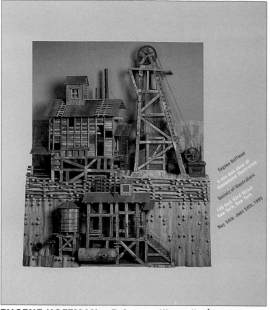

EUGENE HOFFMAN 3-D Art - 26" x 31" $10.00

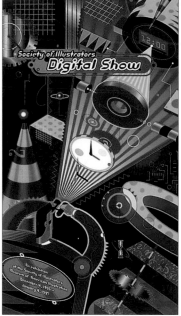

**THE DIGITAL SHOW - Steve Lyons
15" x 27" $10.00**

EDWIN AUSTIN ABBEY 25" x 22" $10.00

39TH ANNUAL - A. Kunz - 22" x 38" $10.00

POSTERS

The Society has created some of the most exciting and enjoyable posters around to announce their exhibitions. Subjects are both contemporary and historic. All are full color and are printed on premium stock.

The set of 7 posters: $40.00

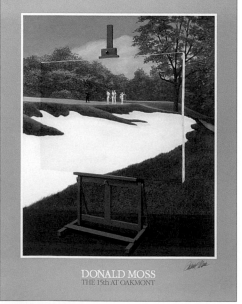

**DONALD MOSS
22" x28"
$10.00**

**40TH ANNUAL
Leo & Diane Dillon
18" x 24" $10.00**

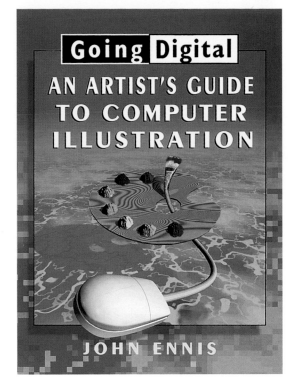

THE BUSINESS OF ILLUSTRATION
Steve Heller's effective text on the nuts and bolts and whys of illustration. Commentary by leading pros and agents as well as hints on pricing and self-promotion. Great for students and young professionals. Recommended highly.
144 pages, softbound, color **$27.50**

GOING DIGITAL
AN ARTIST'S GUIDE TO COMPUTER ILLUSTRATION
At last, an easy-to-read guide to illustrating on your computer. Author and illustrator, John Ennis, offers an under- the-hood look at how it's done and how to start up your digital studio.
144 pages, softbound, color. **$29.95**

HEALTH HAZARDS MANUAL
A comprehensive review of materials and supplies, from fixatives to pigments, airbrushes to solvents.
132 pages, softbound. **$9.95**

THE BUSINESS LIBRARY

Each of these volumes is a valuable asset to the professional artist whether established or just starting out. Together they form a solid base for your business.

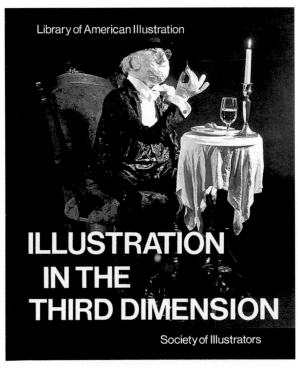

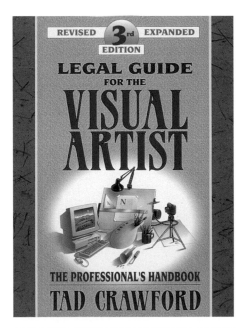

ILLUSTRATION IN THE THIRD DIMENSION
27 artists explain just how dimensional art works. Media include woods, metals, fabrics, resins and junk. This 1978 classic is still an effective look at this genre.
112 pages, hardbound, limited color. **$12.00**

THE LEGAL GUIDE FOR THE VISUAL ARTIST
1997 EDITION.
Tad Crawford's text explains basic copyrights, moral rights, the sale of rights, taxation, business accounting and the legal support groups available to artists.
256 pages, softbound. **$18.95**

GRAPHIC ARTISTS GUILD HANDBOOK PRICING AND ETHICAL GUIDELINES - VOL. 9
Includes an outline of ethical standards and business practices, as well as price ranges for hundreds of uses and sample contracts.
312 page, softbound. **$24.95**

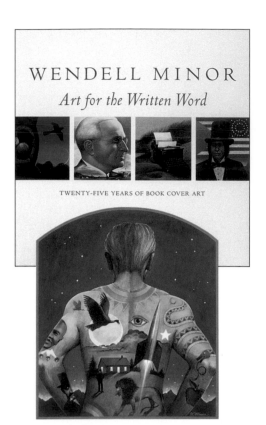

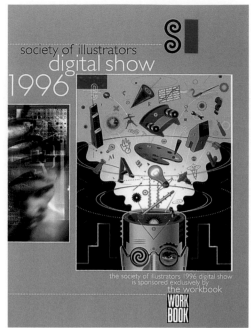

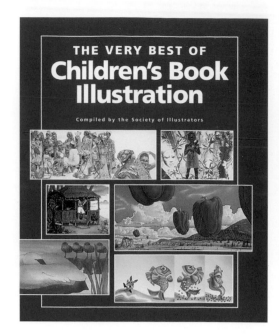

WENDALL MINOR
ART FOR THE WRITTEN WORD
A retrospective of this award-winning artist's book cover art. Includes an introduction by David McCullough and commentary by the authors.
154 pages, color, softbound. **$30.00**

SI DIGITAL SHOW
The Society's 1996 exhibition of the computer as media. 44 current artists show a wide range of stylistic approaches using different software and hardware. Includes Show Chairs and Jurors comments.
36 pages, color, softbound. **$10.00**

A retrospective of Illustrated children's books from 1992. This volume contains valuable "how-to" comments from the artists as well as a publishers directory. A compilation of the exhibition, "The Original Art 1992 - Celebrating the Fine Art of Children's Book Illustration."
136 pages, color, hardbound. **$29.95**

BOOKS & CATALOGS

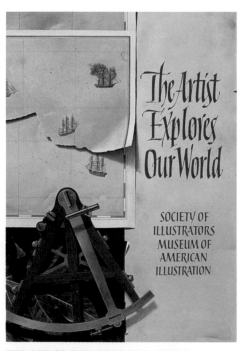

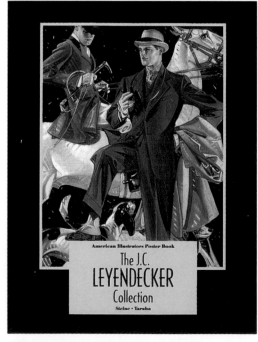

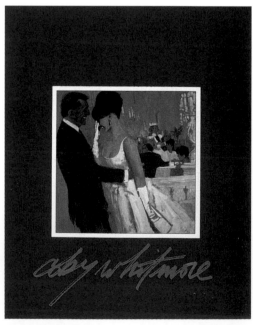

THE ARTIST EXPLORES OUR WORLD
The catalog of National Geographic's Centennial Exhibition. Includes biographical sketches of 44 artists and color samples of most.
16 pages, color, softbound. **$10.00**

THE J. C. LEYENDECKER COLLECTION
Collector's Press poster edition offering 18 plates all from the original art with accompanying text by Fred Taraba. An outstanding addition for the discerning collector.
22 pages, color. 10" x 14". **$24.95**

COBY WHITMORE
The good life of the 1950s and 1960s as illustrated in the Ladies Home Journal, McCall's and Redbook.
12 pages, color, softbound. **$16.00**

APPAREL

SI CAPS
Blue or Red with SI logo and name embroidered in white.
Adjustable,
one size fits all
$15.

White shirt with the Society logo.
L, XL, XXL **$15.**

39TH ANNUAL EXHIBITION "CALL" T-SHIRT
Image of the tattooed face by Anita Kunz.
100% cotton. Heavyweight pocket T.
L, XL, XXL **$15.**

38TH ANNUAL EXHIBITION "CALL" T-SHIRT
Image of a frog on a palette by Jack Unruh.
Frog on front pocket.
100% cotton. Heavyweight pocket T.
L, XL, XXL **$15.**

SWEATSHIRTS
Blue with white lettering of multiple logos or grey with large red SI.
L, XL, XXL **$20.**

40TH ANNUAL EXHIBITION "CALL" T-SHIRT
Image of "The Messenger" by Leo and Diane Dillon.
100% cotton. Heavyweight pocket T.
L, XL, XXL **$15.**

GIFT ITEMS

SI LAPEL PINS
Actual Size
$6.00

The Society's famous Red and Black logo, designed by Bradbury Thompson, is featured on many items.

SI TOTE BAGS
Heavyweight, white canvas bags are 14" high with the two-color logo **$15.00**

SI PATCH
White with blue lettering and piping - 4" wide
$4.00

SI CERAMIC COFFEE MUGS
Heavyweight 14 oz. mugs feature the Society's logo or original illustrations from the Permanent Collection.
1. John Held, Jr.'s "Flapper";
2. Norman Rockwell's "Dover Coach";
3. J. C. Leyendecker's "Easter";
4. Charles Dana Gibson's "Gibson Girl"
5. SI Logo
$6.00 each

SI NOTE CARDS
Norman Rockwell greeting cards, 3-7/8" x 8-5/8", inside blank, great for all occasions. Includes 100% rag envelopes

10 CARDS - $10.00	
20 CARDS - $18.00	
50 CARDS - $35.00	
100 CARDS - $60.00	

ORDER FORM

Mail: The Museum Shop, Society of Illustrators, 128 East 63rd Street, New York, NY 10021-7303
Phone: 1-800-SI-MUSEUM (1-800-746-8738) Fax: 1-212-838-2561 EMail: society@societyillustrators.org

40

NAME _____

COMPANY _____

STREET _____
(No P.O. Box numbers please)

CITY _____

STATE _____ ZIP _____

PHONE ( ) _____

Enclosed is my check for $ _____
Make checks payable to SOCIETY OF ILLUSTRATORS

Please charge my credit card:
☐ American Express   ☐ Master Card   ☐ Visa

CARD NUMBER _____

SIGNATURE _____ EXPIRATION DATE _____
*please note if name appearing on the card is different than the mailing name.

QTY	DESCRIPTION	SIZE	COLOR	PRICE	TOTAL

# of items ordered		Total price of item(s) ordered	
		TAX (NYS Residents add 8 1/4%)	
		UPS Shipping per order	6.00
		or	
		Foreign Shipping per order	15.00
		or	
Ship via FEDEX Economy and charge my account _____			FX
		TOTAL DUE	

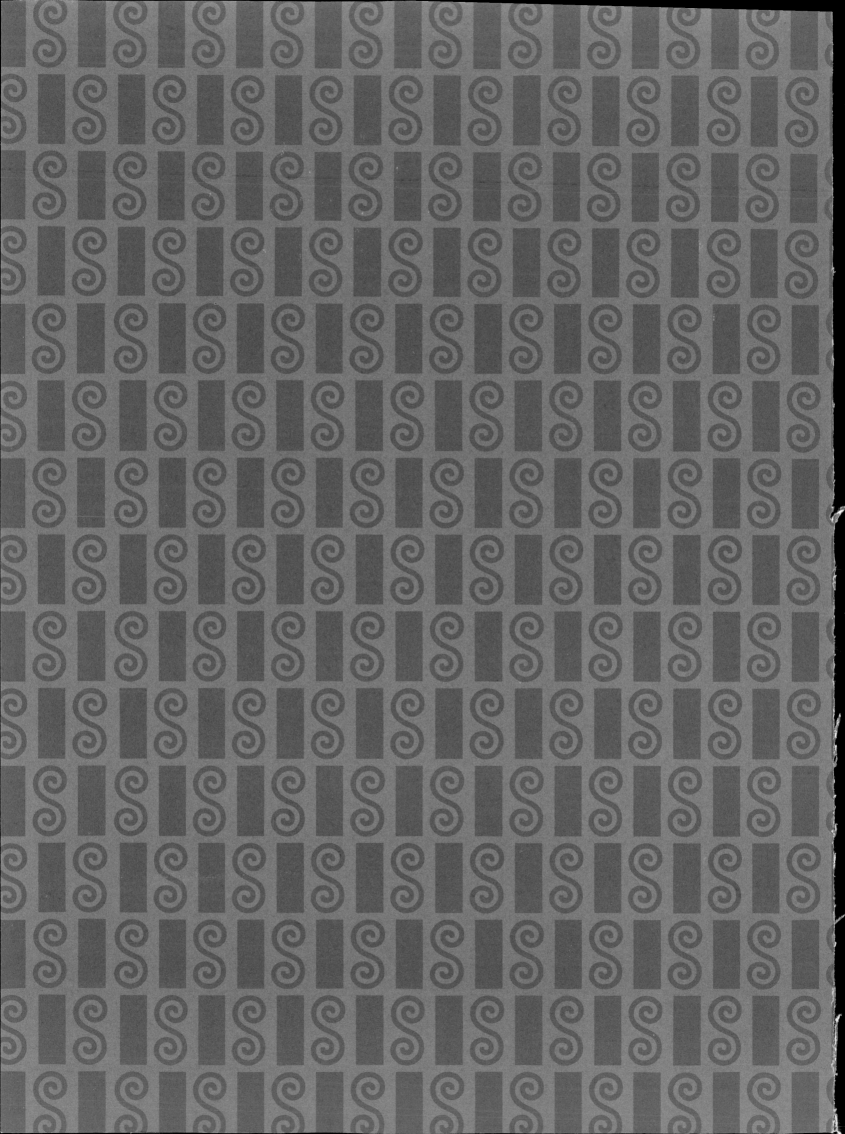